BACK TO SCHOOL ACTIVITY FUN

Publications International, Ltd.

Contributing Writers: Rita Hoppert, Ed.D., Phyllis J. Perry, Ed.D., Peter Rillero, Ph.D., Donna Shryer, Stan and Shea Zukowski

Contributing Consultant: Joseph Peters, Ph.D.

Front and Back Cover: Brian Warling Photography

Contributing Illustrators: Terri and Joe Chicko, Jim Connolly, Yoshi Miyake, Ellen Joy Sasaki

Manufactured in U.S.A.

8 7 6 5 4 3 2 1

ISBN 0-7853-2512-3

How to BRUSH

1 Place brush at angle along outer gumline. Wiggle gently back and forth. Repeat for each tooth.

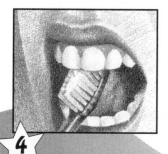

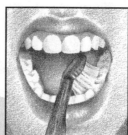

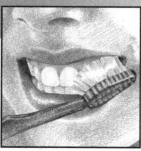

2 Brush inside surface of each tooth, using wiggling technique in Step 1.

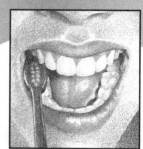

3 Brush chewing surface of each tooth.

4 Use tip of brush to brush behind each front tooth, both top and bottom.

5 Don't forget to brush your tongue!

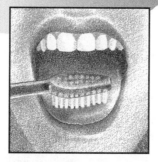

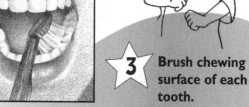

Visit **KIDS WORLD** at Colgate's Web Site!
http://www.colgate.com

CONTENTS

Introduction • 6

Science Activities • 8

Curly Fish • Bottled Sea: Catch a Wave • Caved-In Can • Top Secret Invisible Ink • Gunk • Shrunken Heads • Solid to Liquid to Solid • Moving Molecules • Pop in a Balloon • Yum! Yum! Yum! • Enough to Make Your Milk Curdle • Spinning Snake • Unspillable Water • Book Blast • Wind Sock • Wing It • Paper Clip Chain • Wind Vane • Paper Airplanes • Filtering Out Dirt • Prisms • Up Periscope • Mixing Lights • Not Just Black and White • Colors at a Distance • Bottle Music • Shadow Clock • Shadow Puppets • A Kaleidoscope • Pinhole Camera • A Kazoo • Rubber Bands • Animal Sounds • Make a Compass • Over the Top • A Simple Telephone • Watch an Ounce Lift a Pound • Path of a Ball • Cutting Water • Bubbles, Bubbles Everywhere • High Bounce • The Come-Back Can • Sticky Balloons • Acid Test • Trickle Down Activity • Down and Dirty • Life on a Brick • Beans in the Dark • Who Needs Dirt? • Can Frost • Hollow Strength • Good Taste • Foil Fleet • Sugar Buzz • Time Capsule • Star Light, Star Bright • Planetarium Presentations • Speck-tral Stars • Tite and Mite

Art Projects • 47

Nature Bookmark • Crazy Putty Dough • Sawdust Clay Dough • Salt & Watercolor Picture • Sculpting Clay Dough • Sculpting Clay Statues • Framed Art • Coiled Bowl • Papier-Mâché Mask • Origami Leap Frog • Flower Explosion • Personal Postcards • Batik T-Shirt • Clay Pencil Holder • Straw-Blown Painting • Quilt

CONTENTS

Picture • Corn Syrup Paint • Decorate a Door • Marble Painting • Papier-Mâché Mash • Splatter Prints • Toothpick Architecture • Pencil Painting • Stationery Set • Bubble Prints • Fancy Flowerpot • Polymer Clay Beads • Sponge Painting • Crayon Sun Catcher • Spin Art • Paint with Texture • Modeling Clay Dough • Spiderweb Pictures • Personalize Your Hats • Card Cutups • Confetti Picture • Cornucopia Copies • Personal Place Mats • Holiday Mobile • Custom Pillowcase • Glitter Jars • Stick Puppets • Scrapbook Binding • Dried Flowers • Diorama • Airplane Flyer • Bird Feeding Station • Leaf Printing • Milk Jug Animals • Self-Portraits • Paper Making • Corner Bookmarks • Wind Chimes • Cereal Box Bookbinding • Paper Lanterns • Box Cars • Four Seasons Tree • Painting in Opposites • Puppet Theater • Sock Puppets • Custom Calender • Decoupage Art Box • Pop-Up Greeting Card • Soap Sculptures • Box Costume • Parrot Piñata • Candle Shield • School Supply Box • Crazy Face • Friendship Bracelets • Rolled Paper Beads • Buckskin • Letter Designs

Games & Puzzles • 92

Scramblers • Exploding Glider • Magnet Maze • Happy Birthday! • Who Am I? • Outer Space Trivia • Don't Bug Me! • Perspectives • Mystery in England • Color Fun • True or False • Mystery in India • Creature Quiz • Tool Kit • Box Count • Blocks Galore • Whose Kite Am I? • Dog Quiz • Fill In • At the Store • What's for Lunch? • Crossword Puzzle • Dog Days • International Signs • Going in Circles • Match-Up Books • Mystery in China • Road Sign Shapes • Felt Story Boards • Line Trace #1 • Golly Wolly • State Match • Inventors Quiz • Mega Matchup • Avalanche Maze • Space Shuttle Mystery • Pirate Ship Maze • Travel Trivia • Line Trace #2 • Zoo Babies • Road Map Mystery • Picture Puns • Ancient Egypt Rebus • True or False • Haunted House Maze • Sports Trivia • Crossed Words • Box Maze • Riddlemaker • Chalkboard Rebus • Cat Quiz • Wacky Words • Rebus Story • Dictionary • Wildlife Trivia • Find the Presents • Morse Code • Uncle Elmer • State Trivia • Geography Quiz • Balloon Badminton

Answers • 139

INTRODUCTION

Back to School Activity Fun is divided into 3 chapters: Science Activities, Art Projects, and Games & Puzzles. All 3 sections will engage your imagination and provide you with hours of fun! Each project includes a list of what you'll need and easy-to-follow instructions. Take the time to go over the instructions carefully. Please note that some activities require adult supervision.

Science Activities

When some people think of science, they think of boring textbooks and complicated formulas. Actually, science is just a way of looking at the world around us and at the things we find in it every day. Science is really just a system created by people to gather and organize information.

The projects and activities in this chapter will help you learn how science describes the world you live in. They will help you learn how to study the world the way scientists do. They will also be a way for you to have fun.

Part of being a scientist is being responsible in what you do. Always use care when doing a project. Don't leave an experiment unattended unless you're sure it is safe to do so. If you have pets or younger brothers and sisters, be sure that the project poses no danger to them. Make sure you always clean up after an experiment and dispose of material properly.

After you pick a project, read the entire project so you know exactly what you'll have to do. Make sure that you have all the materials you will need. Most of the projects in this book use items you can find in your house. Also, make sure that you have time to do the project you select. Some projects can be done in just a few minutes, but others have to sit for hours, days, or even weeks, and you'll need to take care of the projects during that time.

Art Projects

Making art projects is a creative and exciting way to keep busy. In each activity, you will learn new skills. You will learn responsibility for your materials and how to clean up after yourself. You will put your creative thinking skills to use as you combine a new idea with another and learn to control the eye and the hand not only for art's sake but also for necessary school skills.

As you try more projects, you'll learn how to use various tools while experimenting with different ideas. A simple project such as paper lanterns can be adapted in size, color, folding technique, and display. You create the additions that make your project unique. Remember, creativity doesn't always mean making something new, it's learning how to combine one idea with another. Many of the projects make great group activities—while you're working on one project, your friend can work on another one. Remember, working together can be fun and doesn't have to be a competition. Work at your own pace and ability level. Help each other choose colors and think of new ideas. Most important, use this time to explore yourself.

You can enjoy arts and crafts all year—for holidays, birthdays, family celebrations, warm days, and even stay-inside days. With a little imagination, there's something here for everyone. This should be an enjoyable, creative experience. Enjoy yourself, have fun, and admire the lasting results!

Games & Puzzles

Games and puzzles come in many different forms, as you will see. The activities in this chapter include classic brainteasers, simple word puzzles, question-and-answer games, interesting trivia quizzes, visual challenges, mazes, and various other exercises designed to be fun and test your problem-solving abilities. These games and puzzles should challenge you, and also included in this chapter are ideas for games and puzzles you can create to challenge your friends and family! Just because you solve one crossword puzzle or learn the answers to a trivia quiz doesn't mean the fun has to end there. You can take what you've learned from that activity and apply it to a whole new puzzle! You will find an "Answers" section at the end of the Games & Puzzles chapter so you can check your answers and get guidance if there is a puzzle you just can't quite figure out.

As the lazy days of summer wind down and school starts up again, you will no doubt be looking for a way to keep your days and weekends filled with fun. *Back to School Activity Fun* will help keep you entertained. Enjoy!

Curly Fish

Warm surfaces expand more quickly than cool surfaces.

WHAT YOU'LL NEED: celluloid; scissors; bowl of water

Cut a simple fish shape from a sheet of celluloid. Your fish should be about 4 inches long and 1 inch wide at the widest part of its body and 1 inch wide from tip to tip of its V-shaped tail. Drop the fish into a bowl of water.

Tell a friend that your fish is so lifelike that if someone picks it up out of the water, it will curl up. When your friend picks up the fish from the water and puts it in his or her hand, probably nothing will happen. But if you rub your two hands together vigorously and then ask your friend to put the fish flat on your open hand, the fish will curl its head and tail together within a few seconds.

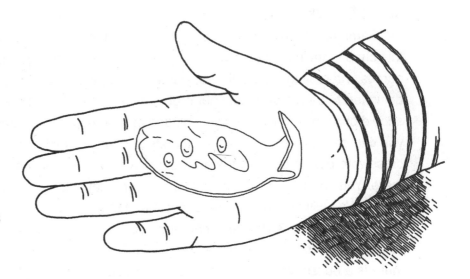

WHAT HAPPENED?

The friction from rubbing your hands together created heat, and the heat was passed on to the fish. However, the plastic fish did not warm evenly. The bottom part touching your warm hand warmed faster and caused the plastic to expand, but the top, colder surface remained the same. This difference in the temperature of the top and bottom sides of the fish caused it to curl.

Bottled Sea: Catch a Wave

Oil and water don't mix—watch the waves build in this experiment.

WHAT YOU'LL NEED: plastic soda bottle; water; blue food color; mineral oil

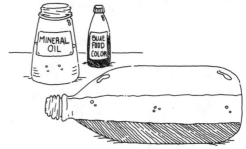

Fill a plastic soda bottle about ⅔ of the way with water. Add blue food color to the water and swirl. Fill the remainder of the bottle with clear mineral oil. Fill it all the way so that no air remains when the bottle is capped. Set the bottle down horizontally, and you'll see a layer of oil on top with a layer of blue water underneath it. Tilt the bottle from side to side slowly, and watch the wave flow. Try tilting 1 side up before the wave reaches it to see the wave crash on shore and reverse directions.

Caved-In Can

Air pressure is strong enough to bend a can.

WHAT YOU'LL NEED: large container; water; ice cubes; empty soda can; measuring cup; stove; tongs or pot holders

Caution: This project requires adult supervision.

Fill a large container with water and ice cubes. Set it aside to use later. Pour ½ cup of water into an empty soda can. With adult supervision, put the can on a burner on the stove. When the water in the can starts to boil, you will see steam coming from the hole in the top of the can. Turn off the stove, and use tongs or pot holders to remove the can from the heat. Quickly put the can in the container of ice water, turning it upside down to rest on its top. Watch as the can cools.

WHAT HAPPENED? When you heated the water in the can, it produced steam that forced the air out of the can. When you put the can in the ice water, its temperature lowered, and the steam condensed back into water. The pressure of the air outside the can was greater than the air pressure inside the can. The weight of the outside air crushed the can.

Top Secret Invisible Ink

Heat can cause a chemical change.

WHAT YOU'LL NEED: toothpick; lemon juice; paper; heat source, such as a lightbulb or iron

Caution: This project requires adult supervision.

Dip the round side of a toothpick into lemon juice, and write a secret message with it on a piece of paper. Use lots of lemon juice for each letter you write. Allow the paper to dry until you can't see the writing any more. Now move the paper back and forth over a heat source. As the ink gets warm, your message is revealed.

WHAT HAPPENED? The acid in the lemon juice breaks down the cellulose of the paper into sugars. The heat supplied tends to caramelize the sugars, making them brown and revealing the secret writing. Repeat this activity with vinegar or milk to find out which makes the best invisible ink.

Gunk

Cornstarch mixed with water has properties of both a liquid and a solid.

WHAT YOU'LL NEED: water; measuring cup; bowl; cornstarch; spoon

Pour 1 cup of water into a bowl. Add cornstarch a little at a time, stirring as you go. You will need about 1½ cups of cornstarch. Keep adding until it gets difficult to stir. When it is perfect, you can hit the solution with your hand and it will not splatter. Have fun with the gunk. Scoop some up, and let it dribble back into the bowl. Try to form some into a ball. Have a friend take a look. Slap your hand into the bowl, and watch as your friend jumps back expecting a splash, but no splash happens. When you've had enough fun with the gunk, throw it in the trash, but don't pour it down the drain, as it may clog the pipes.

Shrunken Heads

Dehydrating—removing water from—a peeled apple is a physical change that causes a change in the size and shape of the apple.

WHAT YOU'LL NEED: apple; potato peeler; knife; string

Caution: This project requires adult supervision.

Peel the skin from an apple with a potato peeler. Using a knife, carve a face into the apple. Hang the apple with a string tied to the stem, and let it dry for 3 days. Observe the shriveled-up appearance of the apple. It has lost water through evaporation. This is a physical change. Observe the face you carved into the apple. It looks shriveled-up like a shrunken head or a witch's face that you could use as a Halloween decoration.

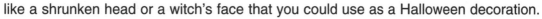

Solid to Liquid to Solid

Solids can change into liquids, and liquids can change into solids.

WHAT YOU'LL NEED: can of frozen orange juice; pitcher; large spoon; water; paper cups; wooden craft sticks

Open a can of frozen orange juice, and spoon it into a large pitcher. Touch the frozen juice to feel that it is both solid and cold. Add water according to the package directions to make orange juice. Fill several paper cups about ⅔ of the way with orange juice. Put a craft stick into the liquid in each paper cup. Being careful not to spill, put the cups of juice into the freezer. Check them after 2 hours. Can you gently pull out the craft stick, or has the liquid orange juice frozen solid around the stick? Once it has frozen, peel off the paper cups. You and your friends can enjoy a frozen treat!

Moving Molecules

The molecules in an object are constantly in motion.

WHAT YOU'LL NEED: 2 glasses; water; food color

Fill a glass with water, and let it sit for a few minutes so the water appears still. Add a couple of drops of food color. Watch as the drops settle to the bottom of the water. Let the glass sit undisturbed for several hours. When you come back, you'll find that the food color has been spread throughout the whole glass of water. Try the project again. This time, use 1 glass of cold water and 1 glass of hot water. Check on the glasses every few minutes. Compare how long it takes the food color to spread throughout the hot water and the cold water.

WHAT HAPPENED? Water molecules are constantly in motion, even if it looks like the water is still. The first time you did the experiment, the moving water molecules collided with the food color molecules and started them moving. After a time, the food color molecules were spread through the glass of water. The second time you did the experiment, you found that the food color spread through the hot water faster than through the cold water. This is because the molecules in hot water move faster than the molecules in cold water. This is true for every substance.

Pop in a Balloon

Gases can dissolve in a liquid.

WHAT YOU'LL NEED: bottle of soda pop; balloon; watch

Open up a bottle of soda pop, and set it on a table. Immediately slip the end of a balloon over the neck of the bottle. Pull the balloon's end well down over the bottle so that it fits tightly. Check on the balloon about every 10 minutes for any changes.

WHAT HAPPENED? Soda pop is carbonated. This means that carbon dioxide gas has been dissolved in the liquid under high pressure. Opening the bottle releases the pressure, and the carbon dioxide gas begins to escape from the liquid. The balloon trapped the carbon dioxide gas as it left the bottle, and then the gas inflated the balloon.

Yum! Yum! Yum!

When liquids evaporate into gases, they can leave material behind.

WHAT YOU'LL NEED: pan; water; stove; sugar; measuring spoon; string; pencil; glass; scissors; button

Caution: This project requires adult supervision.

Bring a small pan of water to a boil on the stove. Turn off the heat. Add 1 tablespoon of sugar, and stir until it dissolves. Continue adding sugar, 1 tablespoon at a time, letting each tablespoonful dissolve completely before adding the next. When no more sugar will dissolve in the water, allow the saturated solution to cool.

Tie a string to the middle of a pencil, and set the pencil across the rim of a glass. Cut the string so that it just touches the bottom of the glass. Tie a button onto the bottom of the string. Pour the cooled sugar water into the glass. Rest the pencil across the rim of the glass so that the string and button are in the solution. Allow it to sit in a warm place without being disturbed for several days so that the water evaporates. As the water evaporates, it will leave sugar crystals on the string. You can eat these crystals; you've made rock candy.

Enough to Make Your Milk Curdle

Acid makes milk curdle. This process is a chemical reaction.

WHAT YOU'LL NEED: vinegar or lemon juice; skim milk; measuring cup and spoon

Place 2 teaspoons of vinegar or lemon juice into ½ cup of skim milk. Stir the milk, and observe the clumps that form. You have just witnessed milk curdling. The proteins in the milk have reacted with the acid and undergone a chemical change.

Spinning Snake

Warm air rises and can cause an object to move.

WHAT YOU'LL NEED: paper plate; markers; scissors; thread

Draw an oval shape in the center of a lightweight paper plate. Starting at the oval, draw a spiral line around and around 4 or 5 times until it reaches the edge of the plate. Use a scissors to cut along the spiral line from the outside edge to the center oval. Draw eyes to make the center oval of the plate into a snake's head. Poke a small hole into the center of the head. Pull a piece of thread through the hole from the top, and tie a big knot in it so the thread will not pull through. Color the snake's body with stripes. Hang the snake by the thread above a heat source, such as a radiator or heating vent. Watch to see what your snake does.

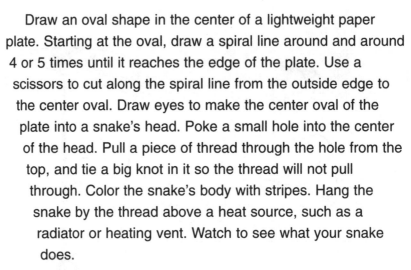

WHAT HAPPENED? Heat from the heat source caused air to rise up toward your snake. As the air molecules bumped into your spiral-shaped snake, they caused it to spin around.

Unspillable Water

Air pressure can be stronger than gravity.

WHAT YOU'LL NEED: juice glass; water; 4×6-inch index card

Fill a juice glass full of water. Let the water run over so that the lip of the glass is wet. Be sure that you fill the glass right up to the top. Place a 4×6-inch index card on top of the full glass of water. Be sure to press the card down securely with your hand so that it makes a good seal all around the wet lip of the glass. Working over a sink, hold the card in place with one hand as you turn over the glass. Carefully let go of the index card. The card will stay in place, and the water will stay in the glass.

WHAT HAPPENED? The force of air pressure against the card was stronger than the force of gravity on the water. The air pressure held the card in place.

Book Blast

Compressed air has great strength.

WHAT YOU'LL NEED: 3 books; large airtight plastic bag

Challenge a friend to move 3 books stacked on top of one another on a table by simply blowing at them. Your friend will be unable to move the books.

Now place a large plastic bag on the table, and put the 3 books on top of the bag. Leave the open end of the bag sticking out over the edge of the table. Hold the opening together, leaving a hole as small as possible. Blow into the bag. Take your time; stop to rest if you need to. If you blow long and hard enough, the books will rise off the table. They will be supported by the compressed air in the plastic bag.

Wind Sock

A wind sock tells you the direction and general strength of the wind.

WHAT YOU'LL NEED: coffee can lid; scissors; cloth; stapler or needle and thread; string; ribbon

Cut the inside from a coffee can lid so that only the rim remains. Put a 15×30-inch piece of cloth over the plastic rim, and secure it by stapling or sewing. The cloth will overlap about 1½ inches. When the cloth is secure around the rim, staple or sew the length of cloth so that you have a long sleeve. Punch 3 holes in the cloth around the rim. Thread a 15-inch piece of string through each hole, and tie each piece securely with a knot around the rim. Tie all 3 strings together about 5 inches in front of the rim. Then tie the ends of all 3 strings together to form a loop, which you'll use to hang your sock from a fence post or tree in the yard. Sew or staple three 1-foot strips of ribbon to the end of the sleeve. Hang the wind sock in an open area in your yard. The wind sock will tell you the direction of the wind. If there is no wind, the sock will hang down limply. If the wind is strong, the sleeve will stand straight out.

Wing It

The shape of a wing gives it lift and allows an airplane to fly.

WHAT YOU'LL NEED: paper; scissors; ruler

Daniel Bernoulli, a Swiss scientist, discovered in 1738 that moving air has less pushing power than still air. This idea, called Bernoulli's principle, is used in the design of airplanes.

To demonstrate the principle, cut a strip of paper 2 inches wide and about 8 inches long. Hold 1 corner of a 2-inch side of the strip in each hand, and hold it just below your lower lip. Gently blow across the strip of paper. You will see that the paper rises.

WHAT HAPPENED? The air you blow over the top of the paper is moving air, so it has less pushing power. The air pressure underneath the strip remains normal. The strong air pressure underneath pushes up and causes the strip of paper to lift. Wings of airplanes are shaped with curved tops to make the air move fast, and the fast-moving air along the top of the wing reduces air pressure and causes lift.

Paper Clip Chain

Magnetism can be passed by induction.

WHAT YOU'LL NEED: strong magnet; paper clips

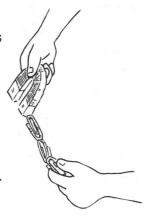

Take a strong magnet, and hold a paper clip to it. Touch a second paper clip to the first one that is hanging from the magnet. The second paper clip will be attracted to the first one because the first clip has become a magnet. Continue adding paper clips in this way to see how long of a chain you can create. Take the first paper clip off the magnet. Do the other paper clips stay joined together, or do they immediately fall?

Wind Vane

A wind vane points into the wind.

WHAT YOU'LL NEED: heavy cardboard; pencil; ruler; scissors; string; nut, bolt, or other weight

Draw a wind vane in the shape of an arrow onto a sheet of heavy cardboard. Your vane should be about 14 inches long and 2 inches wide, and the tail should be wider than the point. Cut the wind vane from the cardboard with scissors. Try to balance your cardboard wind vane on the point of a pencil, and mark the spot on the wind vane where it balances. Punch 2 holes into the wind vane at this balance spot; each hole should be ½ inch from the edge of the vane. Tie an 18-inch piece of string through the top hole and a 12-inch piece of string through the bottom hole. Tie

a nut or bolt to the bottom piece of string for weight. Tie the top piece of string to a tree branch where the vane can swing easily without hitting anything. When the wind blows, your wind vane will point directly into the wind. The larger surface of the tail provides more resistance to the wind and causes the point to face into the wind.

Paper Airplanes

Shape is a factor in how well things fly through the air.

WHAT YOU'LL NEED: paper; tape measure; pen

Throw a flat sheet of notebook paper as far as you can, and then measure the distance it traveled. Try several times, and write down the greatest distance it traveled. Now wad the sheet of paper into a ball. Throw it several times, and measure the distance it traveled each time. Write down the greatest distance it traveled.

Take another sheet of notebook paper. Fold it into an airplane, such as the one shown below. Throw the airplane several times. Does it travel farther than the other sheets you threw? Experiment with different designs for your plane. Which works best?

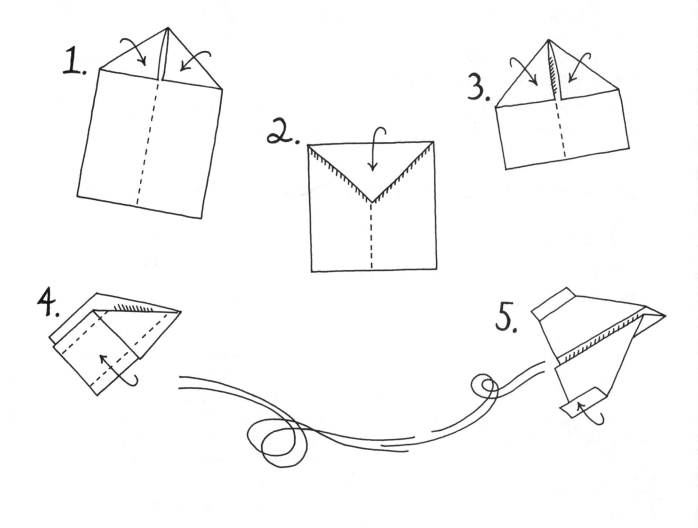

• •

Filtering Out Dirt

You can filter suspended matter from water by using a wick.

WHAT YOU'LL NEED: 8-inch-tall cardboard box; 2 bowls; water; dirt; wool yarn

Set an 8-inch-tall cardboard box on a table. Set a bowl of clean water on top of the box. Gently drop a small handful of dirt into the water. Much of the dirt will remain suspended in the water, and the water in the bowl will be discolored.

Set an empty bowl on the table right next to the cardboard box. Twist together several 1-foot strands of wool yarn to make a rope. Put 1 end of this rope, or wick, into the bottom of the bowl of dirty water. Place the other end of the wick in the empty bowl. After a while, drops of clear water will drip off of the free end of the wick into the empty bowl.

WHAT HAPPENED? The material in your rope absorbs water and draws it from the bowl. It leaves the dirt behind, however, so the water that drips into the second bowl is clean.

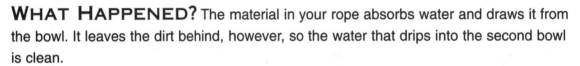

Prisms

White light is composed of all the rainbow colors.

WHAT YOU'LL NEED: scissors; cardboard; prism; white paper

Cut a slit in a large piece of cardboard. Place the cardboard in a sunny window so that a shaft of sunlight shines through the slit. In one hand, hold a prism in front of the cardboard so that the sunlight passes through it. With your other hand, hold a sheet of white paper so that the light passing through the prism shines on it. You will see a rainbow of colors on the paper.

Up Periscope

Air weighs less than water and can be used to make an object float.

WHAT YOU'LL NEED: plastic bottle with a narrow neck; scissors; adhesive tape; 4 quarters; plastic tubing; modeling clay; bathtub filled with water

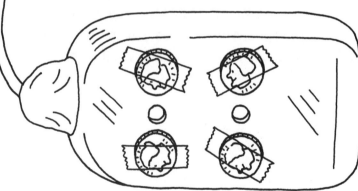

Cut 2 small holes, one above the other, in the side of a plastic bottle, such as an empty shampoo bottle. With adhesive tape, firmly attach 2 quarters on either side of both holes. Put a piece of plastic tubing like the kind that is used in aquariums into the neck of the bottle. Securely seal the opening of the bottle around the tubing with modeling clay.

Lower your submarine into a bathtub of water, keeping 1 end of the tubing above water. Hold your sub under the water until it fills up with water and sinks. Now blow through the end of the plastic tubing. As you blow, you will force air into the submarine and force water out the holes. As the submarine fills with air, it will rise to the surface. By blowing in or releasing air through the tubing, you can cause your submarine to rise or sink.

WHAT HAPPENED?

Air weighs less than water. When your submarine is filled with water, it is more dense and it sinks. When it is filled with air, it is less dense and it floats. Real submarines move up and down in the water in the same way.

Mixing Lights

You can mix colored light to produce new colors.

WHAT YOU'LL NEED: 12-inch square box; scissors; ruler; a cord with a plug at one end and a socket at the other; lightbulb; black paper; red, blue, and green cellophane; tape; white paper; mirror

Cut a few holes in the top of a 12-inch square box to let out heat. Cut a square 3 inches wide and 5 inches high in 1 side of the box; the bottom of the square should be 1 inch above the bottom of the box. Cut a hole in the other end of the box big enough for a lightbulb to go through. Put the socket through the hole and into the box, and screw the lightbulb into the socket.

Cut out a 4×6-inch piece of black paper; cut 3 vertical rectangles that are each 2 inches tall and ¾ inches wide in the black paper. Tape a strip of red cellophane over the left-most hole; tape a strip of blue cellophane over the center hole; tape a strip of green cellophane over the right-most hole. Tape the black paper with the color filters over the square you cut in the side of the box. Put a sheet of white paper on the table in front of the filters.

Plug in the light cord, and then turn out the lights in the room. The light from your box will shine through the filters onto the white paper, showing red, blue, and green light. Use a mirror to reflect the red light onto the green light. What color do you create? Now reflect the blue light onto the green light. What color do you create? What other colors can you mix to form new colors?

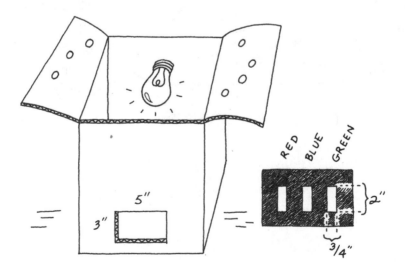

Not Just Black and White

Different colors will be seen when you view spinning black-and-white circles.

WHAT YOU'LL NEED: pencil; ruler; scissors; white paper; black paper; glue; black marker; tape; knitting needle; paper plate

Draw and cut out 3 circles of white paper that are each 5½ inches in diameter. Put a small hole in the center of each circle. Draw and cut out a circle of black paper that is 5½ inches in diameter. Cut the black circle in half. Cut 1 of the halves in half.

Use these materials to make several different disks. Glue a black half-circle onto a white circle so that the disk is ½ black and ½ white. Glue a black quarter-circle onto a white circle so that the disk is ¼ black and ¾ white. Using a black marker, divide 1 white disk into 8 pie-wedge shapes. Color some of the pie wedges black, leaving others white.

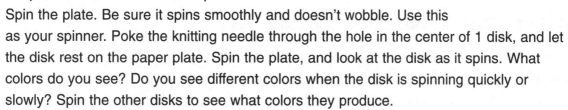

Wrap some tape around the middle of a knitting needle. Put the knitting needle through the middle of a 6-inch paper plate, and push the plate down to rest on the tape. Spin the plate. Be sure it spins smoothly and doesn't wobble. Use this as your spinner. Poke the knitting needle through the hole in the center of 1 disk, and let the disk rest on the paper plate. Spin the plate, and look at the disk as it spins. What colors do you see? Do you see different colors when the disk is spinning quickly or slowly? Spin the other disks to see what colors they produce.

Colors At a Distance

Some colors are more easily recognized than others by the human eye.

WHAT YOU'LL NEED: cloth strips; coat hanger; string; paper; pencil

Ask a friend to tie narrow strips of different-colored cloth to the bottom of a coat hanger so that the strips hang down neatly. Have your friend hang the coat hanger on a tree limb some distance from you.

Divide a sheet of paper into 2 columns. Write your name at the top of 1 column and your friend's name at the top of the other column. Down the left side, list the colors of your strips of cloth: yellow, orange, red, green, blue, black, and so on. When your friend says that the coat hanger is ready to be viewed, carry the sheet of paper and your pen, and walk toward the strips of cloth. As soon as you can see a color, write the number "1" on the paper under your name and next to the color you see to indicate that you saw that color first. Continue numbering all the colors as you see them. Now let your friend have a turn. Do you both agree on which color you were able to see first? Try the experiment again at a different time of day when the light is different. Compare your results to your first experiment.

Bottle Music

When you blow across a bottle, the air inside vibrates and produces sound.

WHAT YOU'LL NEED: 8 empty bottles; water

Stand 8 empty bottles side by side on a table in front of you. Fill the bottle on the left about ¼ of the way full with water. Add water to the next bottle so that the water level is a bit higher than in the first bottle. Continue adding water to the bottles so that each one has a little bit more water in it than the bottle to its left. Blow across the bottle on the left, and you'll hear a low note. Blow across the bottle on the right, and you'll hear a high note. By adjusting the amount of water in each bottle, you can produce a whole musical scale.

WHAT HAPPENED? When you blow across the bottle, you cause the air inside to vibrate, which produces a sound. The amount of air in the bottle affects the sound it makes. The bottles with more air produce low sounds, and the bottles with less air produce high sounds.

Shadow Clock

When rays of light are blocked by an object, a shadow is produced.

WHAT YOU'LL NEED: chalk; watch or clock

On a sunny morning, draw an arrow with chalk on your patio or driveway. Ask a friend to stand facing in the direction of the arrow with 1 foot on either side of the arrow. Now trace around your friend's shadow with chalk. Is it a long or short shadow? Is it in front of your friend or behind your friend? Inside the shadow, write down the time.

Every 2 hours, ask your friend to come back and stand in the same spot. Each time, trace around your friend's shadow, and write the time inside this shadow.

At the end of the day, look at the shadow tracings. Why are some shadows in front of where your friend stood and some behind? Why are some shadows small and some long?

Shadow Puppets

When rays of light are blocked by an object, a shadow is formed.

WHAT YOU'LL NEED: construction paper; scissors; tape; wooden sticks; cassette and cassette recorder; sheet; 2 flashlights

With a couple of friends, plan a shadow puppet show to share with family or other friends. Cut puppet shapes out of construction paper. For Halloween, for example, you might cut out the shape of a witch, a cat, a ghost, and so on. To do a woodland story, you might cut out simple shapes of a deer, rabbit, bird, and squirrel. Tape each of your puppet shapes onto a thin stick of wood so that they will be easy to hold. The nearer the object is to the light, the bigger the shadow will be.

Plan the story you are going to tell, and record it into a tape recorder. You can include background music if you want. Tape a sheet across a doorway. When it is show time, the audience will sit on one side of the door while the puppeteers sit on the other side. Turn on the tape. While 2 friends shine flashlights at the drape, operate the stick puppets in front of the flashlights. The audience will see the shadows of the puppets on the sheet in the doorway.

A Kaleidoscope

Mirrors reflect multiple images off of one another.

WHAT YOU'LL NEED: 3 small mirrors of the same size; tape; waxed paper; pencil; scissors; construction paper

To make a kaleidoscope, tape together 3 small mirrors in a triangle shape with the mirror-sides facing inward. Stand the mirrors up on a piece of waxed paper, and trace around the bottom of the mirrors. Cut out this triangle shape, and then tape the piece of waxed paper in place at the bottom of the 3 mirrors. Cut out many small pieces and shapes from colored sheets of construction paper, and drop them inside the mirrors. Give your kaleidoscope a shake, then look inside. You will see some interesting patterns. The mirrors will reflect interesting shapes and colors.

Pinhole Camera

The image in a pinhole camera is upside down.

WHAT YOU'LL NEED: scissors; empty oatmeal box; aluminum foil; tape; needle; tissue paper

Cut a 1-inch square in the bottom of an empty oatmeal box. Tape a piece of aluminum foil over the 1-inch square. Prick a hole in the middle of the aluminum foil using a fine needle. Tape a piece of tissue paper over the open end of the oatmeal box. On a bright, sunny day, point the box at a house or tree across the street. Look through the pinhole. You will be able to see an image of the house or tree on the piece of tissue paper, but the image will be upside down.

A Kazoo

Vibrating air against paper will make a musical sound.

WHAT YOU'LL NEED: waxed paper; tube from a roll of paper towels; rubber band; pen

Stretch a 4-inch square of waxed paper over 1 end of a cardboard tube from a roll of paper towels. Put a rubber band around the tube to hold the waxed paper in place. Use a pen point to poke a hole in the tube about 1½ inches from the covered end of the tube. Now hold the open end of the tube to your mouth, and hum a tune into it. The waxed paper will vibrate and hum your tune along with you.

Rubber Bands

The rate at which something vibrates determines the sound that it makes.

WHAT YOU'LL NEED: 3 long rubber bands; cardboard box

Stretch 3 rubber bands around a small, sturdy cardboard box that is about 8 inches square and 2 inches deep. Space the rubber bands about 2 inches apart.

Pluck each of the rubber bands. Do they make a sound? Do they sound alike? Pull the middle rubber band tighter, and tie a knot to shorten it a little. Pull 1 of the other rubber bands very tight, and tie a knot to shorten it. Pluck the rubber bands again. Which one produces the highest sound? Which one produces the lowest sound?

WHAT HAPPENED? By pulling the rubber bands tighter, you changed the rate at which they vibrate. The change in vibration rate caused a change in the sound they made.

Animal Sounds

By varying vibrations, you can create animal sounds.

WHAT YOU'LL NEED: scissors; 1-quart milk carton; string; paper towel; water

Cut through a 1-quart milk carton 4 inches from the bottom. Using scissors, punch a small hole in the center of the bottom of the carton, and thread the end of a 24-inch piece of strong string through the hole. Tie several knots on top of each other to make a large knot that will not pull through the hole.

Wet a paper towel, squeezing out the excess water. Hold the milk carton in 1 hand, and put the wet paper towel around the string about 10 inches from the carton. Give the wet towel a quick pull while pressing it with your fingers. It will make a squawking noise that is amplified by the milk carton.

By varying how much string you leave between the wet towel and the box, you will be able to produce sounds resembling a rooster's crow and a lion's roar.

Make a Compass

A magnet that can turn freely will align itself with Earth's magnetic field and point north.

WHAT YOU'LL NEED: large tub of water; bar magnet; clean styrofoam meat tray; scissors

Set a big tub of water on a wooden table. Place a bar magnet in the middle of a small piece of styrofoam that you have cut from a clean meat tray. Set the styrofoam on top of the water in the middle of the big tub. Be sure there is no metal in the area.

Allow the tray to float freely so it can find its own direction. The tray will turn until one end of the magnet points north. The magnet is acting like a compass needle.

Over the Top

You can stretch the surface of water.

WHAT YOU'LL NEED: small plastic cup; water; eyedropper

Fill a small plastic cup all the way to the top with water. Hold an eyedropper filled with water close to the surface of the water in the plastic cup, and gently release the water drop by drop. How many drops can you add to the plastic cup after it is "full"? Can you see that the water level actually rises above the top of the cup? Water molecules attract one another strongly so that the water holds together.

A Simple Telephone

Sound travels through string better than it travels through the air.

WHAT YOU'LL NEED: pen, nail, or other pointed object; 2 hard-plastic containers (such as cottage cheese containers); string

Use a pen to punch a small hole in the middle of the bottom of each of 2 hard-plastic containers, such as cottage cheese containers. Thread 1 end of a 12-foot piece of string through the hole in each container so that the end is inside the container. Tie knots in each end so the string will not pull out through the hole.

Hold 1 cup, and give the other to a friend. Walk far enough apart so the string between the cups is pulled tight. The string should not be touching anything except the plastic containers. Ask your friend to hold the cup over 1 ear while you whisper into the other cup.

Your voice will make the string vibrate. The vibration will travel along the string to the other cup, and your friend will clearly hear what you whispered. Now listen while your friend whispers. Build other phones that use different lengths of string and different kinds of containers, and compare how well they work.

Watch an Ounce Lift a Pound

Centrifugal force increases with an increase in speed.

WHAT YOU'LL NEED: fishing line; empty cotton spool; a 1-ounce object; a 1-pound rock

Thread a 5-foot piece of fishing line through an empty cotton spool. At 1 end, securely fasten the 1-ounce object so that it can be whirled about without danger. Fasten a 1-pound rock to the other end of the fishing line.

Grip the spool so that you are also holding the string beneath it. Let the heavy rock dangle down about 10 inches. Rotate the light object in a horizontal circle above your head. When the light object is spinning around fast, you can release your grip on the string below the spool. As you continue to spin the light object, you will see the heavy object begin to rise on the string that goes through the spool. (Be sure to use a strong line and fasten objects securely so that the objects don't fly off!)

WHAT HAPPENED? Some of the energy you used to spin the light object around generated a centrifugal force that caused the object to move in a circle. As you applied more energy, the centrifugal force became strong enough to lift the heavy object.

Path of a Ball

A ball will bounce off a wall at an angle equal to the angle at which it struck the wall.

WHAT YOU'LL NEED: small ball; wall

Take a small ball with a good bounce, and throw it straight at a smooth wall. Watch the ball carefully. If it hits the wall straight on, it will bounce straight back to you. Now move to the side so you can throw the ball so that it hits the wall at an angle. Watch the ball carefully. It will not bounce back to you; instead it will bounce off the wall at an angle equal to the angle at which it struck the wall. Move to another spot where you can throw the ball so that it hits the wall at an even sharper angle. Again watch the path of the ball. It will be equal to the sharp angle at which the ball struck the wall.

Cutting Water

You can split a water drop into smaller drops, and you can put small water drops together.

WHAT YOU'LL NEED: food color; glass; water; spoon; eyedropper; waxed paper; toothpick; drinking straw

Put a drop of food color into a glass of water; stir until all of the water is evenly colored. Using an eyedropper, gently put several drops of the colored water onto a sheet of waxed paper. Look at the circular shape of the drops.

With a toothpick, try to cut a water drop in half. Can you do it? With a drinking straw, blow gently to try to put 2 water drops together. Can you do it?

WHAT HAPPENED? The surface tension of water pulls the water molecules in a drop toward each other; the molecules in the outer layer are drawn in toward the center of the drop, giving the drop its round shape. The surface tension that holds the water in that shape affected how the water acted when you exerted force on it with the toothpick and the straw.

Bubbles, Bubbles Everywhere

Bubbles get their shape from surface tension.

WHAT YOU'LL NEED: dishwashing liquid; measuring cup and spoon; glycerin; water; large container; dishpan; pipe cleaners; plastic soda pop ring; scissors; stapler; wooden sticks

Add ½ cup of dishwashing liquid and 2 teaspoons of glycerin to ½ gallon of water in a large container. Mix the materials together, and let them sit overnight. The next day, pour the mixture into a plastic dishpan outdoors. Shape pipe cleaners into circles of different sizes. Cut a circle of plastic from a soda pop ring, and staple it to a wooden stick. Dip these devices into the bubble solution, and gently blow through the circles to make bubbles. Circles of different sizes will make bubbles of different sizes.

High Bounce

The force of gravity can be converted to energy.

WHAT YOU'LL NEED: balls of various sizes and materials; pencil; graph paper; large sheet of cardboard; tape measure

Collect some different balls (tennis ball, beach ball, softball, rubber ball, football, basketball, golf ball, etc.). Make a graph that has the names of the different balls across the bottom and height in feet along the sides.

Test the different balls to see which one bounces best on a concrete floor, porch, or driveway. Drop them 1 at a time from the same height in front of a large sheet of cardboard, and mark on the cardboard how high each one bounced. Measure each bounce, and indicate it on your graph.

WHAT HAPPENED? All the balls gained the same amount of energy when they fell. When they struck the ground, the downward force from gravity was converted into upward force that worked against gravity to send the ball up in the air. The different materials and sizes of the balls affected how well each one could convert the energy into upward force, and that affected how high each ball bounced.

The Come-Back Can

You can use the principles of potential and kinetic energy to make a can that seems to change direction on its own.

WHAT YOU'LL NEED: hammer; nail; empty coffee can with lid; weight, such as a washer, nut, or bolt; 2 dowels; rubber band

Use a hammer and nail to poke a hole in the center of the bottom of a coffee can. Use the nail to poke a hole in the center of the coffee can lid as well. Tie a weight, such as a washer, nut, or bolt, to the middle of a rubber band. Put the rubber band through the hole in the bottom of the can so that 1 loop of the rubber band sticks outside the can and the rest of the rubber band (and the weight) is inside the can. Put a dowel through the loop to hold it in place on the outside of the can. Put the other end of the rubber band through the lid from the inside so that a small loop of rubber band sticks out of the lid. Put the other

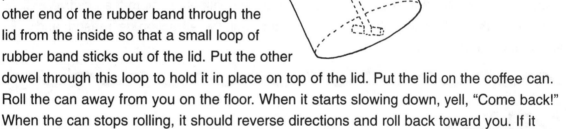

dowel through this loop to hold it in place on top of the lid. Put the lid on the coffee can. Roll the can away from you on the floor. When it starts slowing down, yell, "Come back!" When the can stops rolling, it should reverse directions and roll back toward you. If it doesn't work, try using a different size rubber band.

WHAT HAPPENED? The rolling can has kinetic energy, or energy of motion. As it rolls, the weight inside remains stationary, causing the rubber band to twist around. The rubber band gains potential energy from the kinetic energy of the can. When the can stops rolling, the rubber band unwinds and converts its potential energy into kinetic energy, sending the can back in the other direction.

Sticky Balloons

A charged object can stick to a neutral object by inducing an opposite charge.

WHAT YOU'LL NEED: cloth (wool, polyester, or nylon); balloon; stopwatch

Rub a cloth on a balloon, or rub a balloon on your hair. Put the balloon up against a wall, and let go. Time how long it stays on the wall. Try different cloths and different wall surfaces to see which makes the balloon stick the longest. Make sure you rub it the same number of times each time you charge it to make the comparisons fair.

WHAT HAPPENED? The balloon rubbed with the cloth became negatively charged. When brought near the wall, the negatively charged balloon repelled electrons in the surface of the wall and created a positive charge on the surface of the wall. Opposite charges attract, so the negative balloon stuck to the positive wall surface. As the balloon lost charge to the air and wall, the attraction decreased, and eventually the balloon fell.

Acid Test

Some rocks and minerals contain calcium carbonate.

WHAT YOU'LL NEED: rocks; small cups; vinegar

Gather several small pieces of different kinds of rock. Place each piece into a different cup. Pour enough vinegar in each container to almost cover the rock. See if the rock starts fizzing. If it does, you'll know that the rock contains calcium carbonate because the acid in the vinegar reacts with calcium carbonate to cause the fizzing. Rocks such as limestone, marble, calcite, and chalk react with the acid in this way. Acid rain can also break down rocks, just as vinegar can. Many ancient buildings and statues are made of marble, and acid rain is causing some of them to slowly dissolve.

Trickle Down Activity

A charged object can curve the path of water trickling from a faucet.

WHAT YOU'LL NEED: balloon or comb; cloth (wool, polyester, or nylon); faucet

Charge a comb or balloon by rubbing it with a cloth. Turn a faucet on so the water falls in a slow, gentle stream. Place the balloon or comb near the falling water and watch how the water acts.

WHAT HAPPENED? By rubbing the balloon or comb, you caused it to have a charge of static electricity. The negative charge of the object acted to repel the negative charge that the moving water had, causing the water to change its path.

Down and Dirty

Soil contains microscopic animals that breathe.

WHAT YOU'LL NEED: garden soil; jar with a lid; limewater (available at a drugstore); small container

Drop a large handful of garden soil into the bottom of a big, empty jar. Pour some limewater into a small container. Note what the limewater looks like. Set the container of limewater, uncovered, inside the large jar so it rests on top of the soil. Tightly screw on the lid of the large jar, and leave it undisturbed. In 2 or 3 days, look at the limewater to see if it has changed in any way.

WHAT HAPPENED? The soil contains many microscopic animals. These animals take in oxygen and release carbon dioxide as a waste product, just as you do when you breathe. The limewater turned a milky color because the carbon dioxide produced by the organisms in the soil combined with the limewater to produce chalk. Your garden soil may contain bacteria, protozoans, and threadlike worms called nematodes.

Life on a Brick

You can grow grass on a brick.

WHAT YOU'LL NEED: nonglazed porous brick; bowl; water; pie tin; grass seed

Many plants can adapt to very difficult growing conditions. Grass seed, for example, can sprout in less than ideal locations. Soak a nonglazed brick overnight in a bowl of water. The next day, put the brick in a pie tin. Set the pie tin in a sunny spot. Pour water over the brick so that it runs down into the tin until the brick is sitting in about ½ inch of water. Sprinkle grass seed on the top of the brick. The grass seed will sprout into plants.

Beans in the Dark

Beans grown in the dark will behave differently than those grown in the light.

WHAT YOU'LL NEED: lima beans; glass; water; 2 plastic foam cups; small rocks; sand; potting soil

Soak 6 lima beans overnight in a glass of water. Take 2 plastic foam cups, and put about 1 inch of small rocks in the bottom of each one. Add 1 inch of sand to each cup, and then add about 4 inches of potting soil to each cup.

Plant the 6 bean seeds, 3 in each cup. Water each cup to keep the soil moist but not wet. Put 1 cup on a sunny windowsill and the other in a dark closet. Check on your beans every day to see how they're growing. Are you surprised by the results?

WHAT HAPPENED? After several days, the plants growing on your windowsill will be healthy and green. The plants in the closet will be very pale, but they might be taller than the other plants. Plant cells have special light receptors. When they don't get enough light, they signal the plant to grow long and thin to seek out a light source. Since the light in the closet is limited, those plants don't produce chlorophyll, which makes plants green and absorbs sunlight to produce food. If you move the pale plants next to the green plants in the window, the pale plants will become green in time.

Who Needs Dirt?

You can grow a sweet potato plant without soil.

WHAT YOU'LL NEED: toothpicks; sweet potato; glass; water

Insert 3 toothpicks around a sweet potato near the large end so they stick out to the sides in different directions. Fill a glass most of the way with water. Put the sweet potato into the glass small-end first, and rest the toothpicks on the rim so they hold up the sweet potato. There should be enough water in the glass so that about ¾ of the sweet potato is covered. Put the jar in a sunny spot for several days. Add water as needed. Soon you will have a beautiful vine growing from the top of the potato.

WHAT HAPPENED? Usually you put a plant into soil to make it grow, but you can grow some plants without soil. When the sweet potato plant was growing with its roots in the water and its leaves in the sun, it produced food through photosynthesis and the stored carbohydrates in the potato. This stored food in the sweet potato provided the energy needed to grow a new plant.

Can Frost

Frost forms because of a change in temperature.

WHAT YOU'LL NEED: small metal can; water; salt; crushed ice

Fill a small metal can ¼ of the way with water. Stir 4 tablespoons of salt into the water. Add enough crushed ice to fill the cup, and stir the solution. Observe what happens on the outside of the can.

WHAT HAPPENED? The cold solution in the can lowered the temperature of the can. When the air outside the can came in contact with the cold can, the air's temperature also dropped. The amount of water vapor the air can hold depends on the air's temperature; it cannot hold as much water when it is cold. The water vapor condensed on the cold can, and the low temperature made the water freeze and form frost on the outside of the can.

Hollow Strength

Long bones are hollow or filled with soft tissue, which helps them to be strong but light.

WHAT YOU'LL NEED: notebook paper; tape; paper plate; measuring cup; wooden blocks or other weights

Roll up a sheet of notebook paper into a tube about 1 inch wide. Tape the tube closed so it doesn't unroll. Repeat twice more so you have 3 paper "bones." Stand the bones up on their ends. Put a paper plate on top of the 3 rolls. The hollow rolls support the plate! Now start adding wooden blocks to the plate. Count how many blocks the plate can hold before it collapses the bones. These bones are strong, so they might be able to hold quite a few blocks.

Roll 3 more sheets of paper as tightly as you can, so there are no hollow sections. These bones use the same amount of paper, but they are much thinner. Stand them on end, and put the plate on top of them. Put blocks on the plate until these bones collapse.

WHAT HAPPENED? The hollow bones were able to support more weight. Having a hollow center gave them a better design and made them stronger. The large bones in your body are also hollow. This makes them strong, so they can support more weight, but light, so it takes less energy to move them.

Good Taste

We have taste thresholds for certain types of taste.

WHAT YOU'LL NEED: measuring cup; 11 plastic cups; water; sugar; salt; paper towels; cotton swabs; paper and pen; tape

Mix 1⅔ cups water and ¼ cup sugar to make a 12.5% sugar solution. Pour this into a plastic cup labeled "12.5% SUGAR." Add ½ cup of this solution to 1½ cups water to make a 3.1% sugar solution, and label it "3.1% SUGAR." Add ½ cup of this to 1½ cups water to make a 0.78% sugar solution, and label it "0.78% SUGAR." Add ½ cup of this to 1½ cups water to make a 0.19% sugar solution, and label it "0.19% SUGAR." Make a series of salt solutions, following the above directions but using salt instead of sugar.

Rinse your mouth with water, and dry your tongue with a paper towel. Keeping the solutions out of your sight, have a friend place a clean cotton swab in one of the solutions and then put it

on the middle of your tongue. Tell your partner if you can taste the solution and if it is sweet or salty. Your partner should write down whether or not you could taste the solution. Rinse your mouth and dry it, and have your partner try a different solution and record your response. Keep doing this until all the solutions are tested. Switch roles with your partner.

Which solutions could you taste, and which could you not taste? What was your threshold for sweet, and what was your threshold for salty? Was salt harder or easier to detect than sugar?

Foil Fleet

The design of a boat will affect how well it can perform.

WHAT YOU'LL NEED: scissors; aluminum foil; large container; water; various small objects

Cut out four 6×6-inch squares of aluminum foil. Fold them into different shapes that will float on water. Put your boats in a container of water to see if they float. Add some small objects, such as toy soldiers, paper clips, or washers, to see if the boats support them. How many objects can each boat support before it sinks? Which boat holds the most? Design boats that will hold more objects.

Sugar Buzz

Carbohydrates are absorbed into the blood at different rates.

WHAT YOU'LL NEED: 2 glasses; corn syrup; red food color; measuring spoon; sugar; flour

Sometimes if you eat too much sugar, your head feels a bit odd and may start to hurt. Some people call this a sugar buzz. This also causes your body to work to remove the sugar from the blood. When all of the sugar is removed, your body is hungry again. Starches do not rush into the blood as quickly as sugar does.

Fill 2 glasses halfway with corn syrup. Add 2 drops of red food color to each glass to make artificial blood. Place 1 teaspoon of sugar on top of the liquid in one glass and 1 teaspoon of flour on top of the liquid in the other glass. Watch how long it takes for the liquid to absorb the sugar and flour.

WHAT HAPPENED? The sugar is absorbed faster than the flour. The sugar is made of small molecules that dissolve faster than the large starch molecules in the flour. When we eat sugar, these small molecules quickly pass into our blood. When we eat starches, the molecules take longer to pass into our blood.

Time Capsule

Time capsules help people in the future understand past cultures.

WHAT YOU'LL NEED: various objects; resealable plastic container; plastic bag; shovel; paper and pen

Gather objects that represent the current year. These can be baseball cards, newspapers, magazines, fashion items, or anything else you can imagine. You might write a letter that tells about yourself, your family, or your community. Put these items into a plastic container, and seal it securely. Put the plastic container into a plastic bag, and tie the bag closed.

Find someplace to bury the time capsule; make sure you have permission to do so. Dig a 3-foot hole in the ground, put your time capsule in, and cover it with dirt. Make a sign, and put it on the ground above the capsule, or make a map to the capsule. On your map or sign, indicate what year the time capsule should be opened. When it is opened, people will find artifacts that will give them some information about how you lived.

Star Light, Star Bright

Some stars appear to be brighter than others.

WHAT YOU'LL NEED: scissors; cardboard; ruler; colored cellophane; tape

Cut four 1×4-inch rectangles next to each other on a piece of cardboard. Tape 1 sheet of cellophane over all 4 rectangles. Then tape cellophane over the last 3

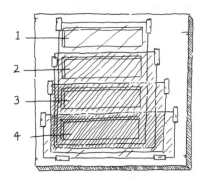

rectangles. Then tape cellophane over the last 2 rectangles and finally over the last rectangle only.

View the night sky with your brightness detector. Notice you can see more stars when you look through fewer cellophane sheets. Only the light from the brightest stars is able to penetrate all 4 sheets. Try to find a star that you can see with 1 sheet but not with 2 sheets. Call this a 1 star. Find a star you can see with 2 sheets but not 3. Call this a 2 star. Find a star you can see with 3 sheets but not 4, and call this a 3 star. Any star you can see through all 4 sheets is a 4 star. Which type of star can you find most often? A star's brightness on Earth depends upon 2 things: the amount of light the star is putting out and how far it is from Earth.

Planetarium Presentations

You can make a representation of the night sky.

WHAT YOU'LL NEED: shoe box; scissors; pen or pencil; pin; tape; flashlight; books

On 1 end of a shoe box, cut a hole just big enough for a flashlight to fit into. Cut a rectangle out of the other end of the shoe box. Draw dots on a piece of paper to represent the stars of a constellation, and poke holes through the dots with a pin; do this for several different constellations. Put 1 of the sheets over the rectangular hole in the box, and tape it in place. Support the flashlight with a stack of books, and put it into the hole in the other end of the box. In a darkened room, turn on the flashlight, and project your constellation onto a wall. Quiz your friends or family to see if they can identify the different constellations.

Speck-tral Stars

Constellations are groups of stars in the sky. They are often given names based on their shape.

WHAT YOU'LL NEED: newspaper; white paper; paint; paintbrush; pencil

Thousands of years ago, people noticed groups of stars and gave them names based on the shapes they seemed to form. Pegasus the Horse, Orion the Hunter, and Ursa Minor the Little Bear all got their names this way. Often, different cultures gave the groups their own names. What we call the Big Dipper, the Vikings called the Wagon, the Chinese called the Emperor's Chariot, and the English called a Plow.

Spread some newspaper over the floor or over a table. Place a sheet of white paper in the middle of the newspaper. Dip a paintbrush into paint. Hold the brush over the paper, and tap your hand so small paint specks fall on the paper. Think of these as stars, and examine them for patterns or shapes you recognize that could be constellations. When the paint has dried, connect the paint specks with a pencil to form shapes you can recognize. Then paint more detailed pictures of the image. Write names for your constellations.

Tite and Mite

Stalactites and stalagmites are deposits of minerals that have been dissolved in water.

WHAT YOU'LL NEED: 2 jars; water; Epsom salts; thick string; paper clips; jar lid

Fill 2 jars halfway with very warm water. Add as much Epsom salts as will dissolve in the water. Attach each end of a 3-foot piece of heavy string to a paper clip. Wet the entire string with the salt solution. Put one end of the string in 1 jar and the other end in the other jar, making sure the ends are covered by the liquid. Let the string hang between the two jars to form a loop. Place a jar lid under the loop. Observe every day for one week.

WHAT HAPPENED? As the string absorbed water from the jars, dissolved minerals from the Epsom salts were carried with the water through the string. They dripped off at the loop. As the water evaporated, the minerals were left behind and formed a stalactite (top) and a stalagmite (bottom). Stalactites and stalagmites form this way in caves when water that contains dissolved calcium drips from the cave ceiling.

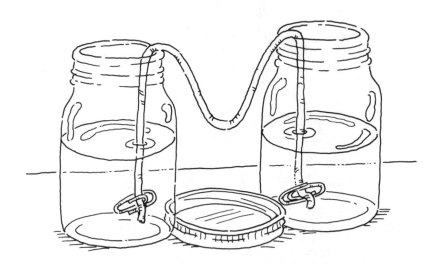

Nature Bookmark

Make a bookmark to remember last summer's garden. Don't forget to include leaves from your vegetable garden as well.

WHAT YOU'LL NEED: 2×6-inch piece of fabric; pressed flowers; craft glue; fabric markers; 2×12-inch piece of iron-on flexible vinyl; iron and ironing board; scissors

Place fabric flat on your work surface with the right side up. Arrange some pressed flowers on the fabric and glue in place. Add more decoration to your design with fabric markers. Let the glue dry. Place the flexible vinyl on the fabric, and slowly peel the paper backing about 2 to 3 inches down from the vinyl. Place the sticky side of the vinyl down at 1 end of the bookmark. Peel the paper backing from the vinyl as you press the vinyl in place on the bookmark. Be sure to keep the edges even. Turn the fabric over to continue pressing the vinyl in place on the back of the bookmark. Once the vinyl is in place, put the paper backing, shiny side down, over the vinyl. With an adult's help, press with an iron for 3 to 4 seconds. Remove the paper and allow to cool. Trim the edges with scissors.

Crazy Putty Dough

With this putty dough, you can make all sorts of silly shapes or magically lift pictures off the funny pages.

WHAT YOU'LL NEED: ⅓ cup liquid starch; baking sheet; craft stick or small spoon; 1 cup craft glue; newspaper comics; drawing paper

Pour liquid starch on a baking sheet. Using a craft stick, slowly stir in craft glue. After it starts to clump, let the mixture set for 5 minutes. Dab a small amount of starch on your fingers and knead the mixture. Now you can pull it, roll it, and stretch it—just like putty!

As you experiment with your homemade putty, use the baking sheet as your work surface. (Be careful not to get putty on the carpet or furniture.) Use the putty to make prints of your favorite comics. Press it on the comic strip, peel it back, and then press the putty on a piece of paper. When you're finished playing with the putty, store it in a small, airtight plastic container.

Sawdust Clay Dough

Bet you thought sawdust was garbage! With this project, you can turn sawdust into wonderful bowls, vases, and even puppets.

WHAT YOU'LL NEED: newspaper; 3 cups sawdust (available at a lumberyard); 2 cups wet wallpaper paste (mix with water according to package directions); acrylic paints; paintbrush

Cover your work surface with newspaper. Mix the sawdust and wet wallpaper paste together in a large bowl, and stir until the mixture becomes doughlike. Take the sawdust mixture out of the bowl, and knead it with your hands.

Use this thick clay to make textural sculptures. You can form your sculpture over a tube, a wire frame, or a small ball of foil. This clay is also great for making small bowls and vases. Once you've finished shaping your clay creation, paint it with a coat of wet wallpaper paste to set it. Let it air dry for about 4 days. When dry, paint it with acrylic paints.

Salt & Watercolor Picture

Salt is great on popcorn, but did you know it's also fun to sprinkle it over a wet painting?

WHAT YOU'LL NEED: newspaper; pencil; drawing paper; watercolor paints; paintbrush; salt

Cover your work surface with newspaper. Sketch a picture, such as a panda bear in a forest, on a piece of drawing paper. Paint the drawing using watercolor paints. While the paint is still wet, sprinkle it with salt. Let it dry. The painting will take on a textured look, and the paper may even crinkle and pucker. You can use this painting technique to make textured backgrounds for holiday cards, stationery, and more.

Sculpting Clay Dough

Ever wondered what a yellow elephant looks like? Or a purple spaceship? Find out when you sculpt and paint your wildest fantasy.

WHAT YOU'LL NEED: saucepan; 1 cup cornstarch; 2 cups baking soda; 1¼ cups water; waxed paper; poster paints; paintbrush

In a saucepan, mix cornstarch, baking soda, and water. With an adult's help, heat it on a medium setting. Stir the mixture continuously until it thickens. Let it cool.

Place a sheet of waxed paper over your work surface. Knead the clay dough for a few minutes. Roll the clay into a ball, and shape it into small sculptures. Pinch ears and legs to make bears, bugs, and bunnies. Let the figures air dry, then paint them using poster paints.

You can also use this homemade clay for the Sculpting Clay Statues project on page 50—just let it air dry instead of baking it. If you want to play with the clay another day, store it in a sealed plastic bag or in an airtight container, and keep it in the refrigerator.

Sculpting Clay Statues

The only difference between a great sculptor and a really great sculptor is imagination. So let yourself go wild!

WHAT YOU'LL NEED: uncoated wire; rolling pin; Sculpting Clay Dough (page 49); aluminum foil; baking sheet, acrylic paints; paintbrush

Make a wire shape base for your clay statue. Create any shape you want—a person, an animal, or even common objects. (Artist Claes Oldenburg copied common household objects such as a can opener for his statues.)

Roll clay into a thin pancake. Place pieces of clay over the wire shape, covering it completely. Use your fingers to smooth over any gaps. Add dimension to your statue by pinching patches of clay over one another or cutting away small areas of clay.

Place your sculpture on a foil-covered baking sheet. To support the shape, crumple some foil pieces and place where needed. Let the sculpture air dry, then paint it with acrylic paints.

Framed Art

This project gives your artwork a finishing touch.
You'll be just like a professional artist in a real gallery.

WHAT YOU'LL NEED: precut colored mat (available at art supply stores; find the size to fit your artwork); craft glue; assorted shapes of dry pasta; assorted colors of glitter and sequins; magnetic strips

Decorate the mat with assorted shapes of pasta or glitter and sequins. Glue them on the frame in a random design; let the glue dry. Cut 4 pieces of magnetic strips and glue them to the back of the mat. Use this decorated mat to display your drawings on the refrigerator. Change your picture as often as you like.

Coiled Bowl

This is truly a bowl of a different color, and it becomes extra special when you make it yourself!

WHAT YOU'LL NEED: assorted colors of polymer clay; waxed paper; scissors; aluminum foil; ovenproof bowl (about the size of a salad bowl); craft knife

Using the palms of your hands, roll clay on waxed paper to make 9 to 10 rolls of clay about 10 inches long. Then roll each clay piece into a circular coil. Cut a circular piece of foil slightly larger than the bowl. Place coiled clay pieces on the foil close together like puzzle pieces. Use your fingers to smooth the surface of the coils until the clay blends together. (Dipping your fingers in water helps to smooth the clay.) Make sure there are no gaps between the pieces. Use a craft knife to trim edges if necessary. Turn the bowl upside down, and turn the clay sheet over onto the bowl with the foil facing out. Press into place. With an adult's help, bake the bowl according to package directions. After the clay has cooled, remove foil and bowl from clay.

Papier-Mâché Mask

Build an original mask out of newspaper strips, and hang your artwork on the wall.

WHAT YOU'LL NEED: newspaper; stapler and staples; 1×4-inch newspaper strips; flour and water (for paste); masking tape; paper rolls or cones; scissors or craft knife; acrylic or poster paints; paintbrush; acrylic sealer (optional)

1. Cover your work surface with newspaper. Fold several sheets of newspaper into long bands. Using the illustration as a guide, make a mask frame (an oval half) with strips of newspaper stapled together.

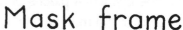

Mask frame

2. Mix flour and water together to make a paste. Use 1 cup of flour for each cup of water. Blend until the paste is smooth. Dip a strip of newspaper in the paste. Rub the strip between your fingers to remove any extra paste. Put the strip over the mask frame and smooth in place. Repeat until the mask is covered with 4 or 5 layers of strips. To add more dimension to your mask, tape on projections before you add the last layer of newspaper strips. Use paper rolls or cones for horns, ears, and a nose. Let the mask dry overnight.

3. With an adult's help, cut out the eyes and a mouth. Paint the mask and let it dry completely. To make your mask shiny, apply a coat of acrylic sealer.

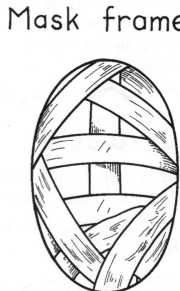

Origami Leap Frog

Origami is the Japanese art of folding paper into objects. Turn a piece of paper into a frog and race it across the table.

WHAT YOU'LL NEED: one 3×5-inch blank index card; pencil

1. Follow the illustrations to fold the index card. Fold point A to point D. Unfold and repeat with the other corner, folding point B to point C. Unfold. Fold the top quarter of the card down and then unfold it.

2. Holding the sides at point E and point F, push them in together toward the center. Press the top half of the paper down, creating a triangle.

3. Fold the point G corner of the triangle up to point I at the top of the triangle, and form a small triangle. Repeat with the other corner of the large triangle at point H.

4. Fold the tiny triangles in half, lengthwise. Then fold each side of the index card in about ¼ inch.

5. Fold the bottom end of the index card up about ¾ inch. Then fold that piece down in half. Turn your frog over, and draw on eyes. Press your finger down at the back of the frog to make it leap.

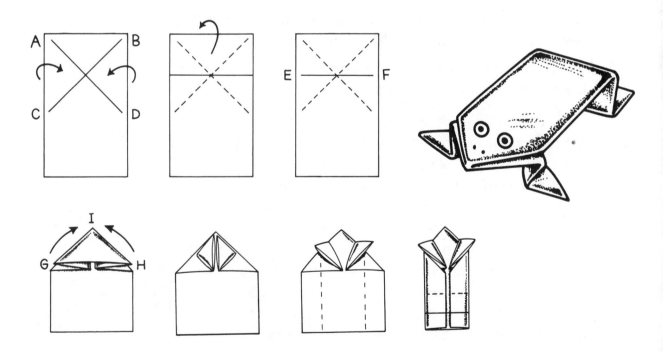

Flower Explosion

If you thought sponges were only for cleaning up messes, you're in for a surprise with this colorful project.

WHAT YOU'LL NEED: construction paper; pencil; scissors; craft glue; heavyweight paper; newspaper; poster paints; paper plates; sponge

Fold a piece of construction paper in half. Draw half of a vase shape at the fold. Cut along the lines of the shape, and unfold the paper. Glue the vase shape on a piece of heavyweight paper.

Cover your work surface with newspaper. Place poster paints on paper plates. Dip a damp sponge in the paint, and then sponge paint "flowers" on the paper above the vase. Twist the sponge to create swirled flowers, or press the sponge on the paper for stamped flowers. You can use this technique to make a bowl of sponged fruit, a tree with sponged leaves, or cornucopia with sponged vegetables.

Personal Postcards

Instead of writing a letter, why not send a personal "hello" to your friends and relatives with handmade postcards?

WHAT YOU'LL NEED: cardstock or 4×6-inch blank index cards; ruler; scissors; black felt-tip pen; colored pencils or markers

Cut a 4×6-inch piece of cardstock. On 1 side of the cardstock, create the back of a postcard. With the ruler, draw a straight line down the center of the card to divide one half for the address and the other half for the greeting. On the half for the address, use a ruler and black felt-tip pen to draw 3 straight horizontal lines from the middle to the bottom of the card. On the other side of the card, create the front of a postcard. Draw yourself at the beach, on a roller coaster, or hiking up a mountain. Your postcard doesn't have to show a real vacation. Draw yourself piloting the space shuttle. Color the picture with colored pencils or markers.

Batik T-Shirt

The great thing about batik T-shirts is that no matter how many you make, each will be different.

WHAT YOU'LL NEED: large plastic bag; white T-shirt; fabric marker or pencil; old crayons; paper cupcake liners; disposable paintbrushes; fabric dye; rubber gloves; paper towels; iron and ironing board

1. Cover your work surface with a large plastic bag. Lightly draw a design on your T-shirt. Remove the paper wrapping from the crayons. Have an adult melt the crayons in paper cupcake liners in the microwave.

2. Paint the melted crayons on your design. Let it dry. Then crumple up the T-shirt. This is what creates the cracked look of batik.

3. With an adult's help, mix the fabric dye according to package directions. Be sure to wear rubber gloves. Soak the T-shirt in the dye for about 10 to 15 minutes. Cover an area of your work surface with paper towels. Place the T-shirt flat on the paper towels to dry.

4. With an adult's help, iron the T-shirt between 4 layers of paper towels. The paper will soak up the excess wax.

crumple

iron

draw

paint

dye

Clay Pencil Holder

This unique holder keeps all your pens and pencils close at hand and neatly organized.

WHAT YOU'LL NEED: assorted colors of polymer clay; waxed paper; rolling pin; butter knife; pen or marker cap; aluminum foil

Roll pancakes of red, orange, yellow, green, blue, and purple clay on waxed paper. Stack them on top of each other in the colors of the rainbow, then use a butter knife to cut them into a 1½×7-inch rectangle. (This will hold about 8 pencils. If you want it to hold more pencils, make the rectangle longer.) Bend the rainbow clay into a big arch with your hands. Using a pen cap, poke a hole in the clay about ¾ inch from 1 end. Make sure it is deep enough to hold a pen or pencil. Make 7 more holes, each about ¾ inch apart. (If you want more pencils in the holder, poke more holes in the longer rectangle.)

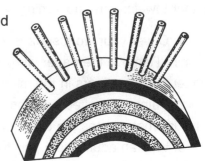

Wad up some foil and place it under the arch for support. With an adult's help, bake the clay arch according to package directions. Once the clay has baked, let it cool and then put your pencils in the holder.

Straw-Blown Painting

Here's a great way to make a splashy picture in wild colors—without even touching the paper!

WHAT YOU'LL NEED: newspaper; removable tape; drawing paper; poster paints; plastic drinking straw

Cover your work surface with newspaper. Tape a piece of drawing paper in the center of your work area. Dilute the poster paint with a little bit of water. Place a small amount of 1 color of diluted poster paint on the drawing paper. Now use your straw to blow the paint around on the paper. Before the paint dries, add another color and blow it around. Let the paints overlap and blend. Try blowing your paint from one corner or out from the center. When you're finished painting, let the paint dry.

Quilt Picture

This looks like an old-fashioned quilt, but there's no sewing and it takes less time than the real thing.

WHAT YOU'LL NEED: pencil; graph paper; ruler; scissors; lightweight cardboard; fabric scraps; old paintbrush; craft glue

Practice drawing your quilt design on a piece of graph paper. Use a ruler to help you draw the triangles and squares of the quilt pattern. Then measure the exact size of the triangles and squares in the design and cut them from cardboard to make the pattern pieces. Place each pattern piece on the fabric scraps and trace around them. Cut out the fabric pieces. Use an old paintbrush to coat the back of each piece with glue. Following the quilt design you drew on graph paper, glue the fabric on the cardboard. After it's dry, trim the cardboard and frame your quilt picture (see Framed Art on page 51).

Corn Syrup Paint

Corn syrup paint dries with a shiny gloss. It almost looks as if the colors are still wet.

WHAT YOU'LL NEED: newspaper; corn syrup; food coloring; plastic egg carton; black crayon; heavyweight white paper; paintbrush

Cover your work surface with newspaper. To make the paint, mix 1 tablespoon of corn syrup with 5 or 6 drops of food coloring in a section of the empty egg carton. Repeat with the other colors of food coloring, keeping each paint mixture in a separate egg carton section.

Using a black crayon, draw a design with thick outlines on a piece of heavyweight white paper. If you draw a baseball player, outline his pants, shirt, arms, and head with thick black crayon lines. Color in each section with the corn syrup paint; don't let the colors touch one another across the black lines. This homemade paint is also great for drawing a jack-o'-lantern or Christmas tree. Since the paint is so shiny, it will seem as if your pictures are all lit up!

Decorate a Door

Turn your bedroom into a magical wonderland. Decorate the door as the entrance to your favorite place.

WHAT YOU'LL NEED: measuring tape; scissors; butcher, wrapping, or mailing paper; markers or poster paints and paintbrush; removable tape; old magazines; craft glue

Measure your bedroom door. Cut out a rectangle the same dimensions as your door from paper. Cut out a hole for the doorknob. Use markers or poster paints to decorate the paper. You can create an underwater scene, a skiing scene, or a giant "do not disturb" sign. Tape it to your door.

If you don't want to draw or paint a scene, make a giant collage for your door decoration. Cut out pictures from old magazines. Glue them to the paper, covering the whole sheet. After the glue has dried, tape the collage to your door.

Marble Painting

You're never boxed in with this unpredictable painting technique. No two designs are ever alike.

WHAT YOU'LL NEED: scissors; drawing paper; cardboard box; removable tape; rubber gloves; marbles; poster paints

Cut a piece of drawing paper to fit the bottom of your box. Tape the paper to the inside bottom of the box. Wearing rubber gloves, dip a marble in poster paint. Place the marble on the paper. Now tilt, wiggle, and twirl the box around to make designs—the marble is your paintbrush! Let the paint dry. Then use more marbles dipped in other colors to add to your design. Experiment with different colors of paper and paint. Start with red paper and make only white marble tracks. Or try black paper with fluorescent-colored paints.

Once all the colors are dry, remove the paper from the box and display your artwork.

Papier-Mâché Mash

This pulpy mash is great for making puppet heads or adding dimension to papier-mâché projects.

WHAT YOU'LL NEED: newspaper; bucket; saucepan; strainer; bowl; craft glue; dry wallpaper paste; aluminum foil; toilet paper tube; sandpaper; acrylic paints; paintbrush

Tear up 4 sheets of newspaper into stamp-size pieces. Place the newspaper pieces in a bucket and soak them in water overnight. After the paper has soaked, have an adult boil the paper and water in a saucepan for 15 minutes. Stir the paper mixture until it is pulpy. Once the mixture has cooled, use a strainer to press out the excess water. Place the paper mixture in a bowl and add 2 tablespoons of glue and 2 tablespoons of dry wallpaper paste. Stir it well until it thickens. Set the mash aside.

To make a puppet head, create a base form with crushed foil. Wrinkle and crush the foil into the head shape you want. Position the shape over the top of the toilet paper tube. Cover the shape with the papier-mâché mash, and sculpt out features. Let it dry overnight. Once it's completely dry, smooth any rough edges with sandpaper, and paint the puppet head with acrylic paints.

Splatter Prints

You're in good shape when you use this terrific painting technique to outline favorite objects.

WHAT YOU'LL NEED: newspaper; drawing paper; large cardboard box; items to outline such as a pressed flower, leaf, or key; old toothbrush; watercolor or poster paints; scissors

Cover your work surface with newspaper. Place a piece of drawing paper in the large cardboard box. Place an item such as a pressed flower on the paper. Dip the bristles of an old toothbrush in watercolor or poster paint. Point the toothbrush down at the paper. Now rub your finger over the bristles toward yourself to splatter the paint around the flower. Remove the flower. The splattered paint looks like confetti outlining your picture. Let the paint dry. To create rainbow splatters, use different colors of paints.

Toothpick Architecture

Create a tiny city, geometric shapes, or a circus tent with clowns. You can build whatever your imagination dreams up.

WHAT YOU'LL NEED: waxed paper; plastic-based clay; flat, round, or colored toothpicks; posterboard

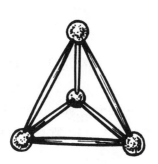

Place a sheet of waxed paper over your work surface. Roll the plastic-based clay into several ¼- to ½-inch balls. (The amount of balls you need will depend on what you're making, since the clay balls are the anchor joints of your toothpick creation.) To make a person, you will need 7 balls of clay; to make a building, you will need 14 balls of clay; and to make a triangle shape, you will need 4 balls of clay. (If you want a permanent structure, use the Modeling Clay Dough on page 66 or the Sculpting Clay Dough on page 49.)

Insert a toothpick into a ball of clay. Connect the toothpick to another ball of clay. Continue connecting toothpicks with the clay until you have completed your structure. Place the finished projects on a piece of posterboard to display your architecture.

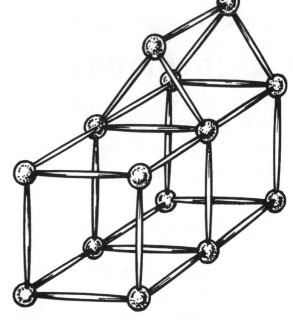

Pencil Painting

Draw a picture and then turn it into a painting with these "magic" pencils.

WHAT YOU'LL NEED: water-soluble colored pencils (available at art supply stores); drawing paper; paintbrush

Draw a lion on a sheet of drawing paper using yellow and brown water-soluble colored pencils. (They feel and look just like colored pencils.) Add big green eyes to your lion. Then wash over your picture using a damp paintbrush. The colors blend just like watercolor paints. Use the paintbrush to blend the colors of the lion's mane. Clean your paintbrush when you change from blending one color to another color.

Water scenes are also fun to paint using these "magic" pencils. Draw a boat at a pier by the lake, using blues for the water. Then use the blending technique to create the boat's reflection in the water. Experiment with other scenes and colors.

Stationery Set

Use these cards to write thank-you letters or to just say "hi" to faraway friends.

WHAT YOU'LL NEED: construction paper; scissors; envelopes; ruled writing paper; craft glue; markers

To make the notecards, cut and fold over a piece of construction paper, making sure it will fit inside the envelope. Unfold the construction paper notecard. Cut a piece of writing paper to fit on the notecard, and glue it in place. Repeat to make a set of notecards. Use markers to decorate each notecard. Draw a simple design such as a series of stripes, curvy lines, or polka dots. Or cut a rippled edge at the bottom of each notecard so a bit of the writing paper shows. This gives the card a lacelike look. Draw a matching design on the envelopes, leaving room for the stamp, address, and your return address.

Grandma+Grandpa
Main St.
Anytown, USA

Bubble Prints

Usually when you blow bubbles, they pop and disappear. Now you can save your bubbles on a piece of paper.

WHAT YOU'LL NEED: ½ cup water; 1 teaspoon dish soap; food coloring; plastic cup; baking sheet; plastic drinking straw; white drawing paper; markers

Mix the water, dish soap, and a few drops of food coloring in a plastic cup. Place the plastic cup on the baking sheet. Place the straw in the cup, and blow bubbles through the straw until they spill all over the baking sheet. Remove the cup and place a piece of paper down over the bubbles. Lift the paper off. The colored bubbles will create a light design on the paper. Let it dry, and then draw in a picture, or outline shapes in the design. Use this bubble-printed paper as wrapping paper, book covers, or stationery.

Fancy Flowerpot

Design your own painted flowerpot to show off a beautiful plant or floral arrangement.

WHAT YOU'LL NEED: clay flowerpot; newspaper; pencil; acrylic paints; paintbrush

Wash the flowerpot, even if it is new, with dish detergent. Rinse it thoroughly, and place it in the sun to dry. Cover your work surface with newspaper. Sketch a pattern or picture on the flowerpot. You can draw an apple pattern, a picture of your family, or an abstract design. Paint it with acrylic paints. Let the paint dry. Once the paint is dry, put a plant in the flowerpot.

Polymer Clay Beads

Use these 4 clay beads—rolled stripe, sculpted, impressed, and marbleized—to make beautiful necklaces and bracelets.

WHAT YOU'LL NEED: waxed paper; assorted colors of polymer clay; single-edged razor blade (use with an adult's help); toothpick; jewelry thread; necklace end clasps

rolled stripe

Place a sheet of waxed paper on your work surface. Choose the beads you want to make, and follow the instructions below. After forming your beads, carefully insert a toothpick through the clay to create a hole. Then have an adult help you bake the beads following package directions. After the beads have cooled, string them on thread, and then tie on the end clasps to complete your necklace.

Rolled Stripe: Use your hands to roll out 2 thin pancakes, each a different color. Cut 1 rectangle from each. Place 1 rectangle on top of the other, then roll up tightly. Slice the roll into beads.

Sculpted: Cut a small circle from clay. Cut tiny pieces of different colors, and press them onto the circle to create a design.

Impressed: Cut a small circle from clay. Press a coin or another object into the circle to create an impression.

Marbleized: Roll out 2 colors of clay. Twist them together and roll into a ball.

sculpted

impressed

Sponge Painting

Use a light technique to sponge paint around your stencils. The result is a perfect background to paint on top of.

WHAT YOU'LL NEED: newspaper; scissors; plastic coffee can lid or plastic plate; cosmetic sponge; assorted colors of stamp pads; drawing paper; colored pencils, crayons, or markers

Cover your work surface with newspaper. Cut out a cloud, a snowflake, or a wave pattern from a plastic coffee can lid. Press a cosmetic sponge on a stamp pad. Place your pattern on a piece of drawing paper and lightly press the inked sponge over the edge of your pattern. Move the pattern around the paper and re-sponge over the edge of it. After you've created your background, let the paint dry. Then draw a scene such as birds in the sky, sleds on the snow, or boats on the sea over the sponge-painted background.

Crayon Sun Catcher

Melted crayons swirl around to become a kaleidoscope of colors, and the bumpy surface makes a wonderful texture.

WHAT YOU'LL NEED: crayons; handheld pencil sharpener; waxed paper; kitchen or bath towel; iron and ironing board; hot pad or oven mitt; scissors; needle and thread

Twist old crayons in a small handheld pencil sharpener to make shavings. Spread them on a sheet of waxed paper, and place another sheet on top. Cover your "sandwich" with a towel. With an adult's help, iron it until the crayons are melted. Remove the towel, and use a hot pad or oven mitt to smooth over the waxed paper. This will spread the crayons, mixing the colors together. After the crayons have cooled, cut the waxed paper into a flower, a star, or any shape you want. To make a hanger, poke a hole through the top of the sun catcher with a needle. String with thread to hang it in your window.

Spin Art

This art project will have your head spinning. Watch as paints mix and swirl to become new colors.

WHAT YOU'LL NEED: nail; cardboard box (with high sides); cork or small wood block and hammer; newspaper; scissors; drawing paper or construction paper; removable tape; poster paints

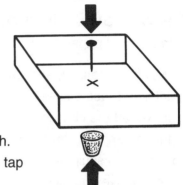

With an adult's help, carefully push a nail through the middle bottom of the cardboard box so that it pokes through. Then push a cork into the nail. (Or use a hammer to gently tap a wood block onto the nail.)

Cover your work surface with newspaper. Cut a piece of paper to fit the bottom of the box. Tape the paper inside the box to hold it in place. Put dabs of slightly watered-down poster paint all over the paper. Hold the cork (or block) and spin the box. The paint will fly toward the sides of the box. Use as many different colors as you want. Untape the paper from the box. Place it on your work surface to dry.

Paint with Texture

Painting with bumpy paint creates a 3-dimensional effect that will make everyone say, "Wow!"

WHAT YOU'LL NEED: newspaper; textured materials such as sawdust, dry coffee grounds, sand, dried herbs, or washed and crushed eggshells; plastic egg carton or small containers; poster paints; pencil; drawing paper; paintbrush

Cover your work surface with newspaper. Place small amounts of textured materials, such as sawdust, in sections of the empty egg carton. Add poster paint in each section and mix.

Draw a picture on a piece of drawing paper. Paint it in with the textured paint. Whether you draw a porcupine or a fire truck, your painting will have a 3-D effect. You can use plain poster paint to create smooth areas of paint on your picture.

Modeling Clay Dough

It's amazing how many interesting shapes you can make with this colorful and fun clay dough.

WHAT YOU'LL NEED: 1 cup flour; ½ cup salt; 1 tablespoon vegetable oil; 1 cup water; waxed paper; food coloring

Mix flour, salt, oil, and water together in a big bowl until the mixture becomes doughlike. Place a sheet of waxed paper on your work surface, and sprinkle it with some flour. Knead the clay dough into a ball on the floured waxed paper. Divide the ball into separate lumps of clay, and add some food coloring to each. Knead each lump well again. Now you can sculpt the clay dough into any shape you want. When you're done sculpting, you can leave your clay creations out to air dry, or store the clay in separate plastic bags or airtight containers. Keep them in the refrigerator until the next time you play.

Spiderweb Pictures

Spiders can be scary, but don't be afraid of these creepy friends. Wherever you put them, that's where they'll stay.

WHAT YOU'LL NEED: construction paper; markers or colored pencils; craft glue; black pom-pom; 2 sequins

Draw a small circle in the middle of a sheet of construction paper. Draw another circle around it. Keep adding bigger circles until you have drawn 4 or 5 circles total. Draw lines from the center circle to the edges of the paper. Draw some lines from the center circle to the edges of the other inner circles. To make the spider, glue a black pom-pom to the web. Glue 2 sequins to the pom-pom for the eyes. Draw in the spider's 8 long legs. If you want, color in all the spaces in the web with bright colors to make it look like a stained glass web.

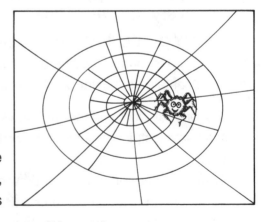

Personalize Your Hats

Turn an old baseball cap into a new, stylish hat of your own. The possibilities are endless.

WHAT YOU'LL NEED: old baseball hat or painter's cap (available at paint supply stores); scrap of fabric; scissors; craft glue; fabric paints; paintbrush; markers; glitter; sequins

Cut a circle or square from a scrap of fabric large enough to cover the front emblem of a baseball hat. Glue the fabric over the emblem. Decorate your hat with fabric paints and markers. Make your baseball hat into a fun beach cap. Paint an underwater ocean scene with fish and seaweed. Use markers to add detail to the picture. Let the paint dry. Glue on glitter and sequins to make the fish sparkle.

Card Cutups

Save your birthday or holiday cards to make card cutups. Use them to create a memory collage, new greeting cards, or special decorations.

WHAT YOU'LL NEED: old greeting cards; scissors; glue; construction paper; markers

Remember your birthday with a memory collage. Cut out the cover designs and inside greetings from old birthday cards. Glue them in a random pattern on a piece of construction paper. Write the date of your birthday on the collage.

To make new greeting cards, fold a piece of construction paper in half. Cut pictures from old greeting cards. Glue them to the front of the construction paper. Then write your own greeting inside.

To make a holiday decoration, cut different pictures from several holiday cards. For example, cut a picture of Santa Claus from one card, a picture of presents from another card, and a tree from a third card. Then glue them together on a piece of paper to make a picture of Santa putting presents under the tree.

Confetti Picture

In this project you will use colored paper dots to create a picture.

WHAT YOU'LL NEED: hole punch; assorted colors of construction paper; pencil; heavyweight paper; craft glue

Punch out dots from different colors of construction paper to make confetti dots. If you want, keep the colors separate in small dishes or containers. Draw a picture, such as a bouquet of flowers, on a piece of paper. Fill in a section of the picture with glue, and sprinkle one color of confetti dots over the glue. Let the glue dry, then shake the paper to remove the excess dots. Continue coloring your picture with more dots. If you want to be more precise, glue single dots in place, one by one, to "paint" your picture.

Cornucopia Copies

A cornucopia is a horn of plenty. Make yours overflow with fruit and flowers, plus plenty of color and texture.

WHAT YOU'LL NEED: pencil; corrugated cardboard; scissors; posterboard; craft glue; newspaper; poster paints; palette or paint tray; small hand-roller (brayer); drawing paper

Draw a horn shape on a piece of corrugated cardboard. Draw fruit shapes such as a pear, a banana, grapes, and apples on cardboard. Carefully peel a layer of paper off the

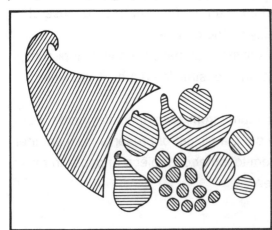

side of the cardboard you have not drawn on to expose the inside ridges. Cut out the shapes. Glue the shapes on a piece of posterboard, ridged side up. Let the glue set.

Cover your work surface with newspaper. Place poster paint on a palette or paint tray. Roll the brayer in the paint, then roll it over the cardboard shapes. Place a piece of paper over the painted surface. Gently rub the paper with your hands. Remove the paper and let the paint dry.

Personal Place Mats

It doesn't even matter if you get these place mats dirty because they wipe clean with a damp sponge. Now that's neat!

WHAT YOU'LL NEED: markers; 12×18-inch piece of posterboard; scissors; cutouts from construction paper or old magazines; craft glue

Use markers to draw a background, such as a beach, on the posterboard. Cut out shapes or pictures from construction paper or old magazines. If you have a beach scene for your background, cut out boats and people. Glue the cutouts on the posterboard. Have an adult take you to a copy center to have your place mat laminated. Leave a ¼-inch border around the place mat.

You can also glue on fun things you want to study, such as maps, sports facts, or poems. Another idea is to draw a maze on your place mat. Once it's laminated, use a grease pencil and play the game again and again.

Holiday Mobile

Let the wind spin and twirl your mobile. It's a great way to see your project from every angle.

WHAT YOU'LL NEED: plastic coffee can lid; scissors; permanent markers; hole punch; string

To make the frame, cut the center from a plastic coffee can lid. Make sure the rim is at least ½ inch wide. Color the rim with permanent markers. To make the hanger, punch 4 holes evenly spaced around the rim. Thread a piece of string through each hole. Bring the ends of each string together at the top and tie them in a knot. Punch 4 more holes between the others. Hang string down from the 4 holes to hold your decorations. Each season of the year, tie on something new: Christmas ornaments, paper Easter eggs, or Halloween ghosts and goblins, for example.

• •

Custom Pillowcase

Stencil on your own custom border to turn a plain pillowcase into something special for your room.

WHAT YOU'LL NEED: pencil; plastic coffee can lids; scissors; plain pillowcase; plastic garbage bag; binder clips; acrylic paints; paper plates; stencil brush

    Draw a flower shape on a plastic coffee can lid. Draw leaf shapes on another coffee can lid. Cut the shapes out to create a flower stencil and a leaf stencil. Put the pillowcase flat on your work surface, and place a plastic garbage bag inside the pillowcase. Place the flower stencil on the edge of the pillowcase, and secure it with a binder clip.

    Pour some acrylic paint on a paper plate. Dip a stencil brush in the paint, and dab off the excess paint on a piece of paper. Dab the brush inside the stencil shape until the shape is filled in. Continue stenciling the flower design along the edge of the pillowcase to make a border. Once the paint has dried, repeat the stenciling process using the leaf stencil and a different color paint. Let the paint dry. If you want, stencil the same border on your bed's dust ruffle or curtains to match your bedroom.

Glitter Jars

Gently shake your glitter jar. Watch what's inside as it swims and floats back to the bottom.

WHAT YOU'LL NEED: white corn syrup; water; small glass jar with a tight fitting lid; food coloring (optional); decorative items such as glitter and sequins; epoxy or super-hold glue; acrylic paints and paintbrush (optional)

Mix corn syrup and water together in the jar. For each 4 ounces of corn syrup, mix in 1 tablespoon of water. If you want to add color to the mixture, put in 1 drop of food coloring. Then add glitter and sequins. You can also add plastic charms such as a little fish to make your jar into an underwater scene. With an adult's help, glue the lid on the jar. Let the glue dry. Decorate the lid and jar using acrylic paints.

Stick Puppets

Turn your life story into a play. Make puppets using your baby photos as well as recent photos.

WHAT YOU'LL NEED: photographs of yourself; scissors; craft sticks; craft glue; cardboard box; poster paints; paintbrush; fabric (to cover the box opening)

Find some pictures of yourself from when you were a baby to the present. Cut out "yourselves" and glue a craft stick to the back of each photo. Make a box stage to act out your play. Cut out the bottom of the box. Decorate the box with paint to make it look like a room in your house. Then tell your own story with your stick puppets. Add a curtain to your stage by gluing a piece of fabric across the top front edge of the box. Pull it back over the top to raise the curtain.

Scrapbook Binding

Save memories from a vacation, jot down your thoughts, or sketch drawings in your own special book.

WHAT YOU'LL NEED: two 11×2-inch pieces of cardboard (for the panel); two 11×12-inch pieces of cardboard (for the covers); two 17×20-inch pieces of cloth; scissors, old paintbrush; craft glue; typing or construction paper; hole punch; yarn

1. Using the illustration as your guide, place 1 cardboard panel piece and 1 cardboard cover piece on 1 piece of cloth. Leave a ¼-inch space between the cardboard pieces. Cut out the corners from the cloth.

2. Remove the cover board from its position, and apply an even coat of glue on one side of the board. Place it back onto the cloth to glue it in place. Repeat with the panel board. Fold the cloth over the boards and glue in place. Let the glue set until dry.

3. Cut a 7×7-inch square from a piece of paper. Glue the square of paper over the cloth edges on the cover board.

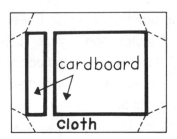

Place cardboard on cloth.

Fold cloth over cardboard.

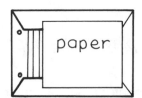

Glue a square of paper over cloth edges.

Tie pieces together.

4. Repeat steps 1 through 3 to make the back cover.

5. Punch 2 holes in the panel of the front and back covers, making sure they line up together. To make the inside pages, punch 2 holes in several sheets of typing or construction paper in the same position as the cover holes. Tie the scrapbook together using yarn.

Dried Flowers

Big bouquets can be used as door decorations or table centerpieces. Tiny bouquets can decorate hats or jewelry.

WHAT YOU'LL NEED: flowers; rubber band; string; hanger; watercolor paints; paintbrush; dish detergent; vase; ribbon

With an adult's permission, gather some flowers from outside. Collect ones that are not quite in full bloom. Gather the stems together and bind them with a rubber band. Thread a piece of string through the rubber band and tie it in a loop. Place the loop over a hanger and hang the bouquet of flowers in the sun upside down. Bring them in at night so dew doesn't collect on them in the morning. Put them back in the sun the next day. They should be dry in about a week. If the sun has bleached out some of the colors, touch the flowers up with watercolor paints. Add a few drops of dish detergent to the paint water to help the paint stick to the flowers. Arrange your bouquet in a vase, or tie a ribbon around it and hang it on the door.

Diorama

A diorama is a miniature 3-dimensional scene with figures or other objects arranged against a painted background.

WHAT YOU'LL NEED: newspaper; shoe box; poster paints; paintbrush; scissors; construction paper; craft glue

Cover your work surface with newspaper. Make a jungle scene on the inside walls of your shoe box. Paint the ceiling blue and the floor brown. Let the paint dry. Cut out trees with a tab at the bottom from construction paper. Cut a small slit in the center of the tab. Fold each tab piece in the opposite direction, and glue the trees standing in the jungle. Put some trees in the back and some in the front of the box to create depth. Cut out jungle animals such as lions, snakes, and monkeys, and glue them in place.

Airplane Flyer

Hang your airplane from the ceiling. If you use fishing line, it looks as if the plane is really flying.

WHAT YOU'LL NEED: pencil or black felt-tip pen; clean foam meat trays; craft knife; permanent markers; craft glue; masking tape

Refer to the illustration and draw the body, wings, and tail pieces of an airplane on a foam meat tray. With an adult's help, cut out the pieces with a craft knife. Decorate them with permanent markers. Cut 2 slots in the body of the plane for the wings and the tail. Insert the wings and tail, adding a dot of glue to hold them in place. Now you're ready to test fly your plane. If you need a weight adjustment in the nose or tail, use some masking tape to add the weight.

Bird Feeding Station

Turn a plastic bottle into something useful—a place for birds to feast.

WHAT YOU'LL NEED: plastic 2-liter bottle (without a base cap); nail; scissors; strong cord; 12-inch wood dowel; birdseed

Soak the bottle in warm water to remove the label. With an adult's help, use a nail to carefully poke a hole in each side of the plastic bottle near the bottom for the perch. Make sure the holes are large enough to fit the dowel. Cut 2 U-shaped cuts 2 inches above each perch hole. Bend them outward like a little awning. Punch 2 holes just under the top rim of the bottle for the hanger. Thread a piece of strong cord through the holes to hang the feeder. Insert the dowel through the perch holes. Fill the feeder with birdseed, and put the cap back on the bottle. Hang the bird feeder outside, and watch the birds eat.

Leaf Printing

Gather leaves to print a pattern or design on notecards. It's surprising how pretty your picture will be.

WHAT YOU'LL NEED: newspaper; light-colored construction paper; fresh leaves; acrylic paints; paintbrush; scrap paper

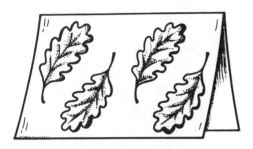

Cover your work surface with newspaper. To make a notecard, fold a piece of construction paper in half. Brush a coat of paint on the back of a leaf. Place the leaf, paint side down, on the front of the notecard. Put a piece of scrap paper over the leaf, and smooth the paper over with your hand. Remove the paper, and carefully peel back the leaf. Let the paint dry. Use more leaves and different colors to create interesting patterns. Continue leaf printing to make more notecards.

Milk Jug Animals

Invent your own animal containers. Create silly features using paper rolls, pipe cleaners, pom-poms, or yarn.

WHAT YOU'LL NEED: plastic milk jug; pencil; scissors or craft knife; permanent markers; craft glue; black pom-pom; scraps of pink and gray felt; posterboard or cardboard

Make a mouse from a plastic milk jug. Draw a cut line on the jug as shown. Then, with an adult's help, cut out the top part of the jug. Leave the handle on to carry your container. Draw on the mouse's eyes and whiskers. Glue on a black pom-pom for the nose. Cut 2 small semicircles from a scrap of pink felt. Glue 1 on each ear. Cut a long tail from the gray felt, and glue it to the back of the jug at the bottom. Draw paws on a piece of posterboard, and cut them out. Glue the paws to the bottom of the jug.

Self-Portraits

If a close friend or grandparent lives far away, make a self-portrait and mail it to them. It's better than a photograph!

WHAT YOU'LL NEED: grocery bags or a roll of brown mailing paper; masking tape; markers; yarn and fabric scraps (optional)

Unroll a long sheet of mailing paper, or cut up 2 or 3 grocery bags and tape them together end to end. Place the sheet down and tape it to hold it in place. Lie down on the paper and have a friend or a family member trace around your body. Now decorate your outline with markers. If you want, glue on yarn for your hair and fabric scraps for your clothes. Make yourself into anything you want. You can be yourself, an astronaut, or a ballerina.

Paper Making

Learn the basics of paper making to create pretty, textural paper for art projects or stationery.

WHAT YOU'LL NEED: junk mail or newspaper; dishpans; blender; 8×8-inch piece of small-holed screening; towels; smooth board (to press the paper); cotton cloth

Tear up junk mail envelopes (without the windows), old letters, or newspaper into small pieces. Soak them overnight in a dishpan with warm water. The next day, add more warm water to the paper, and hand-beat the mixture until the pulp is broken apart. Or use a blender to mix it. Place the soaked paper in a blender, and fill it half full with water. With an adult's help, blend it in short bursts to break the pulp up.

Spread some pulp evenly on the screen. The screen should be covered with the paper pulp. Place the screen on a towel. Press a board down hard on the paper to squeeze out any excess water. Remove the board. Place a piece of cotton cloth on a flat surface. Turn the screen over onto the cloth to remove the paper. Let the paper dry.

Corner Bookmarks

When Mom calls you for dinner and it's time to stop reading, use your own bookmarker to hold your place.

WHAT YOU'LL NEED: junk mail envelopes; scissors or pinking shears; markers or colored pencils; scrap of felt; craft glue

Cut the corners from the envelopes of your junk mail. For a straight edge, use scissors to cut the corners. If you want a zigzag edge, use pinking shears. Decorate each corner triangle with markers or colored pencils. Draw on eyes, ears, whiskers, and a nose to make a bookmark mouse. Cut a little tail from a scrap of felt, and glue it to the back of the bookmark. If you cut a wavy edge on the corner triangle, draw a sea scene on the bookmark. Draw waves and a sailboat. Place the triangle bookmark on a page corner to mark your place in your book.

Wind Chimes

Hang your wind chime outside and listen to its sounds. It's as if the soft breezes are singing to you.

WHAT YOU'LL NEED: plastic coffee can lid; scissors; string; plastic egg carton; large jingle bells

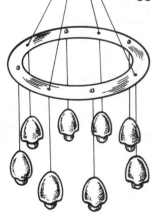

To make the wind chime ring, cut the center from a plastic coffee can lid. Make sure the ring is at least ½ inch wide. To make the wind chime hanger, punch 4 holes evenly spaced around the ring. Thread a piece of string through each hole. Bring the ends of each string together at the top, and tie them in a knot. Punch 4 more holes between the others. Hang string down from each hole on the ring.

Make egg carton bells for each string. Cut out a cup, and poke a hole in the center. Thread the cup through the hanging string, and tie a jingle bell into each cup.

Cereal Box Bookbinding

Create your own journal, scrapbook, or sketchbook. Now you have a place to put precious memories.

WHAT YOU'LL NEED: typing paper; needle and thread; empty cereal box; scissors; two 9×11-inch pieces of wrapping paper; craft glue; white construction paper

1. Fold 40 sheets of typing paper in half. Separate 8 sheets from the 40, and sew the pages together along the fold using a needle and thread. Repeat with 4 more 8-page sections. Cut the front and back covers from a cereal box. Follow the cut lines shown in the illustration to cut two 6×9-inch pieces with a ½-inch spine.

2. Place a 9×11-inch piece of wrapping paper on your work surface, and cut off the corners as shown. Coat the front cover piece with glue, and place it down on the wrapping paper. Glue the flaps over. Repeat for the back cover.

3. Cut two 5×7-inch pieces of white construction paper. Glue 1 to the inside of each cover piece. Glue the spines of the front and back covers together. Then put glue on the inside spine, and insert the five 8-page sections. Let it set overnight.

Wrapping paper

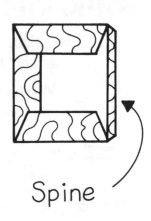

Spine

Paper Lanterns

String a series of pretty paper lanterns along an outside porch or window. Watch them sway gently in the wind.

WHAT YOU'LL NEED: wrapping paper or construction paper; scissors; transparent tape

1. Cut a 4×6-inch piece of paper. Fold the rectangle in half lengthwise. Cut slits along the fold about ½ inch apart.

2. Open the paper and tape the short edges together with the fold pointing outward.

3. Cut a strip of paper to make a handle. Tape it across the top of the lantern. Now you can hang your lantern. Make more lanterns so you can hang a series of them outside or in your room.

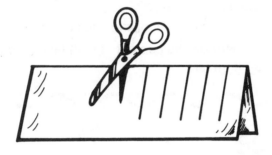

Make cuts in the fold.

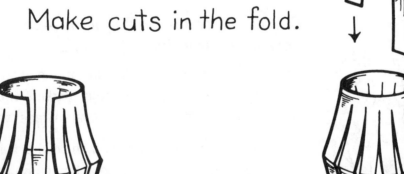

Tape short edges together.

Tape handle across the top of the lantern.

Box Cars

With a few materials and a little imagination, you can make a race car, a sports car, or even a minivan.

WHAT YOU'LL NEED: old boxes; construction paper; craft glue; markers; plastic milk jug lids; cardboard; scissors; clear plastic cup; aluminum foil

Save some small boxes from the kitchen or from gifts about the size of a butter box, a cocoa mix box, or a necklace box. Cover the boxes with different colors of construction paper. Decorate paper-covered boxes with markers. For the wheels, glue on plastic milk jug lids or cut circles from cardboard. Make a windshield from a clear plastic cup cut in half. Glue it to the box. Use aluminum foil to make headlights and bumpers.

Four Seasons Tree

Don't wait for the next holiday—celebrate now with a tree for all seasons.

WHAT YOU'LL NEED: thin tree branches or twigs; construction paper; scissors; markers or colored pencils; lightweight string or transparent tape; vase

Find 4 similar-size branches with several twigs coming off of them. Decorate each branch with the coloring of winter, spring, summer, and fall. Cut snowflakes, flowers, bugs, and leaves from construction paper. Decorate them with markers or colored pencils. Tie or tape the shapes on each branch for each of the 4 seasons. Arrange the branches in a pretty vase to make a colorful centerpiece for a table.

Painting in Opposites

Every color has an opposite, or complementary, color. Use the opposite color of what's expected and create a surprising world.

WHAT YOU'LL NEED: pencil or colored pencils; drawing paper; ruler; newspaper; watercolor or poster paints; paintbrush

Do you know which colors are the primary colors? They are red, blue, and yellow. Which colors are the secondary colors? Mixing the primary colors creates the secondary colors. They are green, orange, and purple. Now that you know which colors are which, draw a color wheel. To create a color wheel, draw a circle on a piece of drawing paper. Use a ruler to divide it into 6 equal "pie" pieces. Label or color in every other "pie" piece as a primary color. Then fill in the opposite secondary colors. Label the "pie" piece opposite of red as the secondary color green. Finish labeling the remaining colors.

Cover your work surface with newspaper. Draw a summer scene of a field with flowers and trees. Paint it in opposite colors. Use your color wheel to pick the opposites. For example, your grass will be red, and the sky will be orange with a purple sun. Let the paint dry.

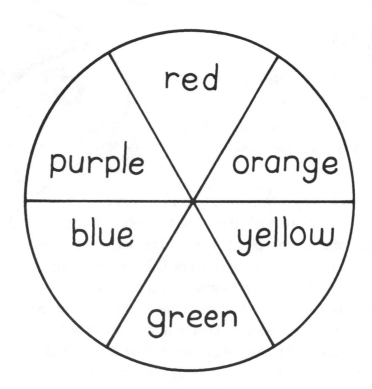

Puppet Theater

With this portable puppet stage you can take your show on the road.

WHAT YOU'LL NEED: 44×44-inch piece of fabric; needle and thread; measuring tape; scissors; fabric paints; two 1×2-inch boards 4 feet long; 8 feet of cord

Fold the fabric in half. Have an adult help you sew the first pocket seam 2 inches below the fold. Then measure 20 inches from the first seam and stitch across the fabric. To make the pocket seam, sew another stitch 2 inches from the previous one. Measure 2½ inches from the top pocket seam, and cut a 25×15-inch hole for the puppets. Decorate the fabric with fabric paint. Let the paint dry. Insert the 1×2-inch boards in each of the 2 pocket seams. Tie the cord from one end of the top bar to the other end. Hang the theater in a doorway, or prop the top bar between 2 chairs.

Sock Puppets

Make a cast of colorful characters with old socks in bright colors.

WHAT YOU'LL NEED: old, clean sock; needle and thread; 2 buttons; fabric markers; scissors; felt; craft glue

Make a dragon sock puppet. With an adult's help, sew on button eyes to your sock. Be sure you don't sew through to the other side. Draw 2 eyelash shapes on a piece of felt and cut them out. Glue the eyelashes to the sock above the button eyes. Draw a mouth and scales on the dragon with markers. Draw and cut out the dragon's tongue, wings, and spikes from the felt. Refer to the illustration, and glue the pieces to the dragon. Make more puppets with other socks. Add trims to make a princess and a knight. Use felt pieces for their clothes and features and yarn for their hair. Now you're ready to put on a puppet show. See Puppet Theater (above) to make a stage.

Custom Calendar

So many things happen in a year! With this calendar you can enjoy a special memory every month.

WHAT YOU'LL NEED: 13 sheets of light-colored construction paper; hole punch; yarn; coloring tools such as colored pencils, markers, or watercolor paints and paintbrush; craft glue (optional)

Gather all 13 sheets of construction paper together. Punch 3 to 5 holes along one long edge. Thread a piece of yarn through the holes. Tie the ends together in a knot and trim any extra yarn. Punch 1 hole at the center of the opposite end. With the holes at the top, decorate the calendar cover.

Think about the types of activities your family or friends take part in each month. Draw a picture for each month, depicting these activities as well as the seasons. Use a different coloring tool for each month. To start, flip the first page. The page at the top (the back of the cover) can be either January or September, depending on whether you want your calender to reflect the calender year or the school year. Decorate the page. Draw the actual calendar on the bottom sheet, copying from another calendar for the dates. Flip the page and do the same for the remaining months. Don't forget to write in special dates like birthdays and holidays.

Decoupage Art Box

Decorate a plain box using fun cutouts. Find pictures of your favorite things, or look for a theme such as dinosaurs, angels, or flowers.

WHAT YOU'LL NEED: newspaper; scissors; wrapping paper or old magazines (for cutouts); wooden box (available at craft stores); craft glue; water; paintbrush; water-based polyurethane

Cover your work surface with newspaper. Carefully cut out the pictures that you want to paste on your box. Once you have gathered all the pictures you will need to decorate your box, position them on the box to create a scene. Dilute some glue with water. Remove the pictures from the box, and coat the back of the pictures with the diluted glue completely and evenly. Press them back onto the box. Smooth out any bubbles. Let it dry. Apply a coat of polyurethane to the box. Let it dry completely, then apply a second coat.

Pop-Up Greeting Card

Give a little extra lift to your message with a special greeting card that springs to life.

WHAT YOU'LL NEED: construction paper; ruler; pencil; scissors; craft glue; markers

1. Fold a piece of construction paper in half. Halfway down the fold, make 2 pencil marks about 2 inches apart. At each mark, cut a slit through the fold 1 inch into the paper.

2. Fold the cut flap back and forth several times to crease it well. Bring the flap back to center. Unfold the page almost completely, and gently push the flap through to the other side. You should have a rectangle that pops out of the paper.

3. Draw a shape or design for your greeting card on another piece of construction paper. Cut it out, and glue it to the front of the pop-out rectangle. Fold another piece of construction paper in half. Trim the pop-up paper so that it is slightly smaller than the second piece of paper. Glue the back of the pop-up paper to the inside of the larger paper. Decorate the front of your greeting card, and write a message inside.

4. If you want to make your pop-up cards into a pop-up gift book, repeat steps 1 and 2 to make several pop-up pages. Then draw and cut out the items for your story from construction paper. Glue those shapes on the pop-up rectangles. Glue the back of one page to the front of another. Repeat this until all the pages are glued together. To make a cover, fold another piece of construction paper in half. Glue the first and last pages inside the cover. Decorate the cover of your book.

Soap Sculptures

Turn routine hand washing into an amusing game with these delightful little soap sculptures.

WHAT YOU'LL NEED: soap flakes; medium-size bowl; spoon; water; food coloring; scented oil (optional); waxed paper

Pour some soap flakes in a medium-size bowl. Gradually stir in water until the mixture reaches a stiff, doughlike consistency. Add a few drops of food coloring to the mixture to make colored soaps. If you want to make scented soaps, add a few drops of scented oil to the batch. Cover your work surface with waxed paper. Place the dough on the waxed paper, and sculpt it into shapes such as shells, butterflies, or hearts. Let them dry overnight. Place them in a gift box, and give them to your friends or family members.

Box Costume

Turn an oversized box into a great Halloween costume. Make animals, cars, buildings, or even furniture!

WHAT YOU'LL NEED: large cardboard box; scissors; markers; newspaper; poster paints; masking tape; wide cloth ribbon; stapler

With an adult's help, cut the bottom and top off of a cardboard box. Use the top and bottom pieces to make a horse's head and tail for a carousel horse costume. Draw the shape of a horse's head and tail on the cardboard pieces. Decorate the shapes with markers, and cut them out. Cover your work surface with newspaper. Paint the horse body with poster paints. After the paint has dried, tape the head and tail to the box body.

Make suspenders to hold the horse costume around your body. With an adult's help, staple a long piece of wide ribbon to one inside corner of the box. Staple the other end of the ribbon to the opposite inside corner. Staple a second piece of ribbon to the inside of the remaining corners so that the ribbon suspenders cross over one another.

Parrot Piñata

A piñata is a decorated container filled with sweet treats. You hit the piñata and when it bursts, everyone gathers the goodies.

WHAT YOU'LL NEED: newspaper; large (12-inch) balloon; flour and water (for paste); scissors; poster paints; paintbrush; markers; posterboard; masking tape; colored tissue paper; craft glue; assorted candy; strong string

Cover balloon with strips.

Cut out parrot head and wings.

Cut a triangular flap to fill the piñata with candy.

1. Cover your work surface with newspaper. Blow up the balloon and knot the end. Mix flour and water together to make a paste. Use 1 cup of flour for each cup of water. Blend until the paste is smooth. Cut 7 or 8 pages of newspaper into 1×4-inch strips. Dip a strip of newspaper in the paste. Rub the strip between your fingers to remove any extra paste. Place the strip over the balloon and smooth in place. Continue covering the whole balloon with a layer of strips, overlapping them slightly. Then apply 3 more layers of strips. Let the balloon dry for a few days. Once it's dry, carefully poke 2 small holes at the top about 4 inches apart.

2. Paint the balloon body in bright colors. Let the paint dry. Draw a parrot head shape and 2 wing shapes on a piece of posterboard. Color them in or add detail with markers. Cut the shapes from posterboard and tape them to the balloon body. Dab paint over the tape to conceal it. Cut long strips of colored tissue paper for the parrot's tail. Glue the tissue paper strips to the balloon body.

3. With an adult's help, cut a 3-inch-wide triangular flap between the 2 top holes. Fold down the flap to remove the balloon and fill the piñata with candy. To make the hanger, thread a piece of string through the 2 top holes and knot the ends. Push the flap back in place.

Candle Shield

Since you can't see the candle behind your shield, it will seem as if your picture is glowing all by itself.

WHAT YOU'LL NEED: heavy-duty aluminum foil; scissors; permanent marker; pushpin; candle

1. Cut three 8-inch squares from the aluminum foil. Place the 3 foil squares on top of each other. Fold the edges over about 1 inch on each side.

2. Use a permanent marker to draw a design, such as a jack-o'-lantern, on the foil. Place the foil on a soft surface such as a rug or a piece of foam. Following the lines of the drawing, punch out the design using a pushpin.

3. Curve the foil so that it stands up about 3 inches in the front of a candle. (Make sure there is a base under the candle to catch wax drips.) Have an adult light the candle.

Fold edges over.

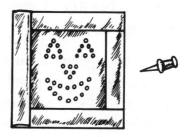

Punch out a design.

Place the shield in front of a candle.

School Supply Box

This special box is perfect for carrying all the crafts, pencils, crayons, and paper that you want to bring with you to school.

WHAT YOU'LL NEED: shoe box; glue stick; scissors; decorating materials (old travel magazines, fabric, different types of paper, markers, stickers)

Let your imagination run wild. Because this is a school box, think about using pictures of pencils, rulers, and maps. Use the most interesting photos you can find as decorations. Glue the decorations to the shoe box.

Crazy Face

Save wear and tear on your own face by making this delightful crazy face do some of the work!

WHAT YOU'LL NEED: 1 white paper plate; scissors; at least 2 strips of white paper (1×11 inches); crayons

Make 4 slits in the top third of the paper plate and 2 slits in the bottom third of your plate, each about 1½ inches long. Thread 1 strip of paper each through the top slits and bottom slits as shown. Don't pull them all the way through.

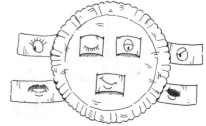

On the top strip of paper, draw a pair of eyes. When you finish that pair, move the strip of paper to the right until they disappear. Now draw a different pair of eyes. Make them mad, glad, goofy, or sleepy. The crazier the better! On the bottom strip of paper, draw different mouths, just as you did for the eyes. When you're finished, move the strips back and forth. How many wacky faces can you make? Make new strips, if you want, or make a new face with 3 rows of slits—one for eyes, one for mouths, and one in the middle for noses!

Friendship Bracelets

Friendship bracelets tell your friends and family how special they are—so make a bunch and give them all away!

WHAT YOU'LL NEED: embroidery floss; scissors; tape (or someone to hold the end for you)

There are many bracelet patterns. This one is so easy it braids itself! Cut 6 pieces of embroidery floss, each 24 inches long. Pick whatever colors you like. Tie the strings together with a knot about 3 inches from the top. Tape the knotted end to a table or wall, or have a friend hold the end for you while you work.

Twist all the pieces together tightly, starting near the knot and moving down (Picture 1). Make a very tight twist about 14 inches long. Leave about 3 inches, and tie the ends together like you did to start. Now hold the end of the twist with one hand. Press down in the middle of the twist with the pointer finger of your other hand (Picture 2). Fold the twist in half, making sure both sides are even.

Take your pointer finger out of the middle, and watch the bracelet braid itself! It's okay if the twist gets bunched up. You can straighten it out. Remove the tape, or have your friend let go of the end. Tie the 2 ends together into a big knot. To wear your bracelet, pull the knot through the loop in the other end of the bracelet (Picture 3).

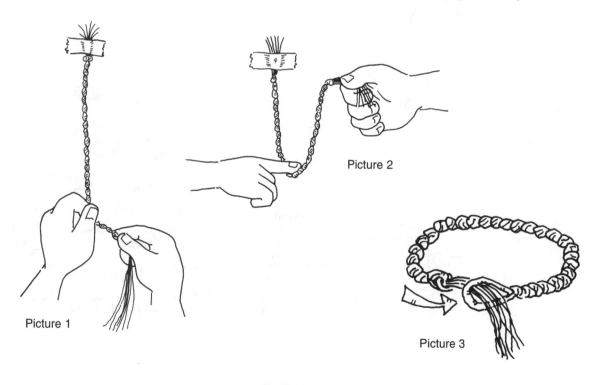

Picture 1

Picture 2

Picture 3

Rolled Paper Beads

Rolled paper beads are colorful and shiny—perfect for making tons of beautiful necklaces and bracelets.

WHAT YOU'LL NEED: old magazines; pencil; ruler; scissors; craft glue; yarn or dental floss; newspaper; acrylic sealer spray

1. Cut out 2 or 3 colorful pages from a magazine. Use a ruler to mark an inch along the long edge of a magazine page. Continue making inch marks along the page. Starting at the first 1-inch mark, cut a long triangle from the magazine page. Repeat until you have 20 to 30 triangles.

2. Starting with the wide end of the triangle, roll it around a pencil. Continue rolling until you reach the point of the triangle. Place a dot of glue at the point. Slide the paper bead off the pencil. Repeat until you've made 20 to 30 beads, depending on how long you want your necklace to be.

3. String the beads on yarn or dental floss. Tie the ends together in a double knot. Spread newspaper over your work surface, and place the necklace on the newspaper. With an adult's help, spray acrylic sealer to give your beads a shiny finish.

Cut out triangle.

Roll a triangle onto a pencil.

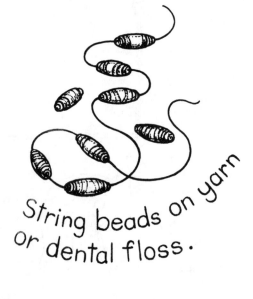

String beads on yarn or dental floss.

Buckskin

Explore the history of Native American symbols by re-creating their beauty on pretend pelts.

WHAT YOU'LL NEED: brown grocery bag; scissors; pencil; pastel chalks; hairspray (optional); craft glue or transparent tape

Cut a brown grocery bag in the shape of a pelt. Crumple up the paper until it becomes very soft. Flatten it, then draw a buffalo, sun and moon, or feathers. Color in the picture using pastel chalks. If you want, have an adult spray it with a very light coat of hairspray to set the chalk.

Another idea is to make a ceremonial shield instead of a buckskin. Cut the brown paper bag in a circle instead of a pelt shape. Crumple the paper, then flatten it and draw a Native American design on the paper. Cut out paper strips to create fringe. Glue or tape the paper strips to the paper circle.

Letter Designs

Use your imagination to make your own personalized nameplate for your bedroom door or create a fun alphabet game.

WHAT YOU'LL NEED: colored pencils or markers; drawing paper; ruler; cardboard; scissors; craft glue; hole punch; yarn

On a piece of drawing paper, draw an object in the shape of its first letter. For example, the word snake starts with an s. Draw a snake in an s shape and then write out the rest of the letters. Color in your letter design. Try making a poster of all the letters in the alphabet with letter designs.

To make a nameplate, cut one 3×8-inch rectangle from a piece of paper and one from cardboard. Draw an object in the shape of each letter in your name on the paper. Then color in each letter design. Glue the paper on the cardboard; then punch a hole in the top 2 corners of the nameplate. String it with a piece of yarn to hang it up on your door.

Scramblers

Sorting out a scrambled puzzle takes real word muscle.

Unscramble the following words. Then, circle individual letters in each word as instructed. Finally, use all of the circled letters to figure out the 2-word answer to the following riddle: What has 4 wheels and flies? (Answers on page 139.)

P R A T
(Circle first 3 letters.)

I G L E G G
(Circle third, fourth, and sixth letters.)

C R A B E
(Circle first 3 letters.)

C U L K Y
(Circle middle 3 letters.)

Making your own scramblers for other people is just as much fun as solving them yourself. It is easiest if you work backward and think of the riddle you want to solve first. Write the answer down, then think of some short words that have those letters in them. Scramble the words and you're done!

Exploding Glider

Here's a project you can throw together quickly. Just be careful to toss your glider away from other people.

WHAT YOU'LL NEED: 6 craft sticks or frozen treat sticks; markers; cardboard (optional)

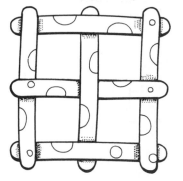

Decorate the sticks with markers. Arrange the sticks in the window pane pattern shown in the illustration. The cross pieces go over and under the outer pieces to provide the tension that holds the sticks together. Now go outside and throw your glider. When you throw it, it explodes! You can make glider games. Draw a big bull's-eye pattern on a piece of cardboard. Place it on the floor. When you throw the glider, add up the points you score as it lands on different sections.

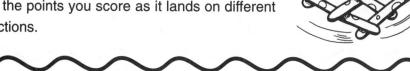

Magnet Maze

The force of magnetism can be exerted through paper.

WHAT YOU'LL NEED: paper plate; pencil; paper clip; bar magnet; timer

Draw an interesting maze with lots of twists and turns and some dead ends on the surface of a large, white paper plate. Make the path of your maze slightly wider than the width of a paper clip. When the maze is finished, ask a friend to hold the plate. Place a paper clip at the start of the maze. Holding a bar magnet beneath the paper plate, try to guide the paper clip through the maze without touching any of the lines. If the paper clip crosses a line, change places, and let your friend try to guide the clip through the maze. You might want to time yourselves to see how long it takes to move through the maze.

Happy Birthday!

Put each word in the grid. Use the letters in the grid to help you.
(Answers on page 139.)

CAKE

CANDLES

CARDS

GAMES

MUSIC

PRESENTS

TOYS

Who Am I?

Have you ever forgotten your own name? You will when you play this guessing game!

Think of a person or character. Pick someone that other players will probably know. We'll use Snow White in our example. The other player will try to guess the person you have chosen. He or she asks, "Who Am I?" You respond by giving clues, one at a time. After each clue, the other person tries to guess the secret identity. Clues for Snow White might be:

1. You have black hair and live in the forest.
2. One of your friends is always in a bad mood. (Grumpy)
3. You get very sleepy after eating an apple.

Keep going until the person who is guessing gets the right answer. To keep score, count the questions and see how long it takes a player to figure out "Who Am I?"

Outer Space Trivia

Here's a trivia quiz that's out of this world. (Answers on page 139.)

1. On April 12, 1961, who became the first human being in outer space?
  A. Alan Shepherd
  B. John Glenn
  C. Gordon Cooper
  D. Yuri Gagarin

2. Who was the first person to walk on the moon in July 1969?
  A. Neil Armstrong
  B. Edwin Aldrin
  C. Michael Collins
  D. Buck Rogers

3. What was the name of the first space shuttle, launched on April 12, 1981?
  A. Enterprise
  B. Queen Mary
  C. Columbia
  D. Titanic

4. What is the largest planet in the solar system?
  A. Earth
  B. Pluto
  C. Venus
  D. Jupiter

5. What planet is closest to the sun?
  A. Venus
  B. Mars
  C. Mercury
  D. Neptune

6. What is the red spot that is visible on the planet Jupiter when you look at it through a telescope?
  A. Meteorite crater
  B. Storm
  C. Lake
  D. Volcano

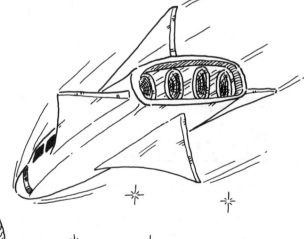

Don't Bug Me!

Each bug on the word list is hidden in the box. Look forward, backward, up, down, and diagonally (on a slant). Circle each one as you find it and cross it off the list. We found HORNET for you. (Answers on page 139.)

WORD LIST

BEETLE

FIREFLY

FLEA

~~HORNET~~

LADYBUG

MOTH

TICK

```
E L T E E B Y
M G A Q L G L
H O R N E T F
G M T G T A E
N Q Z H B F R
A T Z C K L I
T I C K Z E F
G U B Y D A L
```

Perspectives

Things can really look different when you change your point of view.

Take a look at the objects on the right. Which one matches the shape on the left drawn from a different angle? (Answer on page 139.)

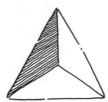

1 2 3 4

Mystery in England

Can you solve your way out of this mystery?

While visiting your uncle, Lord Wisenberry of Eaglethorpe, in his English mansion, you decide to go exploring. In the basement, you accidentally lock yourself in a dusty storage room. There's only 1 door and no windows. The door key is hanging on a hook high on the wall, but no matter how much you jump, you can't reach it. You try calling for help, but everyone is at the other end of the mansion.

The only items in the room are a deck of playing cards with the king of spades missing, a broken cardboard box holding a set of 24 encyclopedias from 1934, and a dirty blue rug. How will you get out of the room? (Give up? See page 139 for the answer.)

Color Fun

Can you put each color word into its spot below? We put in a few letters to start you off. (Answers on page 140.)

BLACK

BLUE

BROWN

GREEN

ORANGE

RED

WHITE

YELLOW

True or False

Read each sentence. If it's TRUE, circle the letter in the TRUE column. If it's FALSE, circle the letter in the FALSE column. Then read the circled letters from top to bottom to find the name of a western state. (Answers on page 140.)

	TRUE	FALSE
Z is the first letter of the alphabet.	E	A
Carrots are orange.	R	S
January is the first month.	I	U
A baby cat is a kitten.	Z	B
Shoes are worn on the hands.	I	O
Marbles are square.	G	N
1 + 1 = 3	O	A

Mystery in India

Can you solve your way out of this mystery?

While adventuring in India, you buy a pet tiger, a pet swan, and a huge bag of cashews to share with your family. Walking back to the hotel, you reach a wide, fast river. The bridge is washed out, but you see a tiny boat. An old man nearby says, "You may borrow my boat to cross the river. But because it is small, you can carry only 1 thing across the river at a time."

Now, you know that tigers hate cashews. But if you leave the tiger and the swan alone together, the tiger will eat the swan. If you leave the swan and the cashews alone together, the swan will eat the cashews. How will you get the tiger, the swan, and the cashews across the river? (Give up? See page 140 for the answer.)

Creature Quiz

Try this monster of a quiz. (Answers on page 140.)

1. In what year was the story Frankenstein written?
   - A. 1985
   - B. 1710
   - C. 1818
   - D. 1936

2. Dr. Jekyll turned into Mr. Hyde the monster after:
   - A. He drank a potion he had made
   - B. A witch put an evil curse on him
   - C. He was struck by lightning
   - D. He read a book about it

3. Godzilla the dinosaur-monster lived in what country?
   - A. United States
   - B. Japan
   - C. Korea
   - D. England

4. The Loch Ness monster is said to live in what country?
   - A. Ireland
   - B. Scotland
   - C. Wales
   - D. England

5. What monster has the body of a lion, the head and wings of an eagle, and the tail of a snake?
   - A. Griffon
   - B. Pegasus
   - C. Centaur
   - D. Medusa

6. This monster guards the tombs of the ancient Egyptian pharaohs. It has the body of a lion, the face of a human, and the wings of a giant bird. What is its name?
   - A. Grendel
   - B. Mothra
   - C. Sphinx
   - D. Gorgon

Tool Kit

Look for the 8 listed things that could be found in a tool kit. Search across, down, and diagonally (on a slant). Circle each word and cross it off the list as you find it. We circled NAIL for you. (Answers on page 140.)

WORD LIST

BOLT

DRILL

FILE

HAMMER

LEVER

~~**NAIL**~~

SAW

WRENCH

```
W  P  X  D  S  V
R  B  K  R  A  L
E  F  O  I  W  E
(N  A  I  L) Q  V
C  J  D  L  T  E
H  A  M  M  E  R
```

Box Count

Quick! It's time to take inventory. How many boxes are stacked in this pile?

You might think it's an impossible task, but you really can count what you cannot see if enough clues are provided. In this case, they have been.

Suppose you were working at a warehouse, and your boss told you he has a client on the phone who will buy all of the boxes—provided that there are at least 80 of them. He needs to know right away. Can you figure it out? (Answer on page 140.)

Blocks Galore

Find the only path through the maze. (Answer on page 141.)

IN   OUT

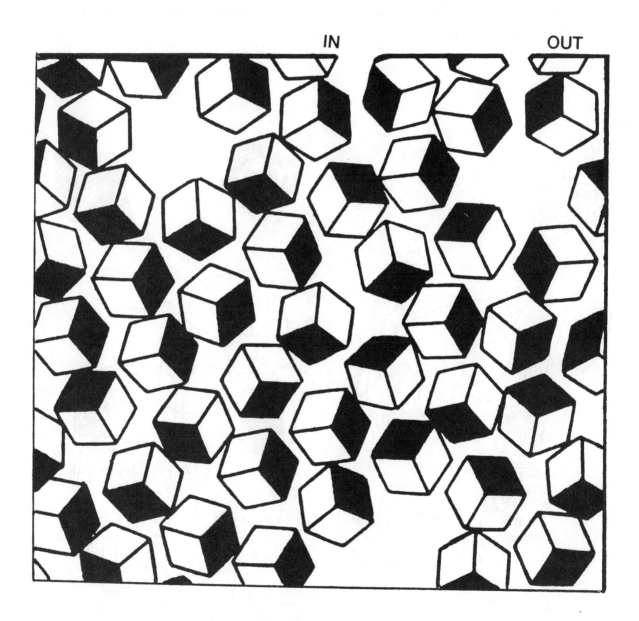

Whose Kite Am I?

See if you can follow the path from each kite to its owner.

What a windy day! These 4 friends were just in the park, flying their kites, when a huge burst of wind tangled them all up. Can you figure out which kite belongs to which person? (Answers on page 141.)

Dog Quiz

How much do you know about "man's best friend"? (Answers on page 141.)

1. Which of the following is a dog's sharpest sense?
   - A. Smell
   - B. Sight
   - C. Touch
   - D. Taste

2. What is the heaviest dog, weighing in at a record 305 pounds?
   - A. Saint Bernard
   - B. Bullmastiff
   - C. Rottweiler
   - D. Great Dane

3. How many teeth does a dog have?
   - A. 36
   - B. 58
   - C. 42
   - D. 28

4. What is the world's fastest dog?
   - A. Irish setter
   - B. Whippet
   - C. Cocker Spaniel
   - D. Greyhound

5. What kind of dog doesn't bark?
   - A. Pekinese
   - B. Dachshund
   - C. Basenji
   - D. Akita

6. What is the smallest breed of dog in the world?
   - A. Schnauzer
   - B. Poodle
   - C. West Highland White Terrier
   - D. Chihuahua

Fill In

Color in only the shapes with dots in them to make a picture. (Answer on page 141.)

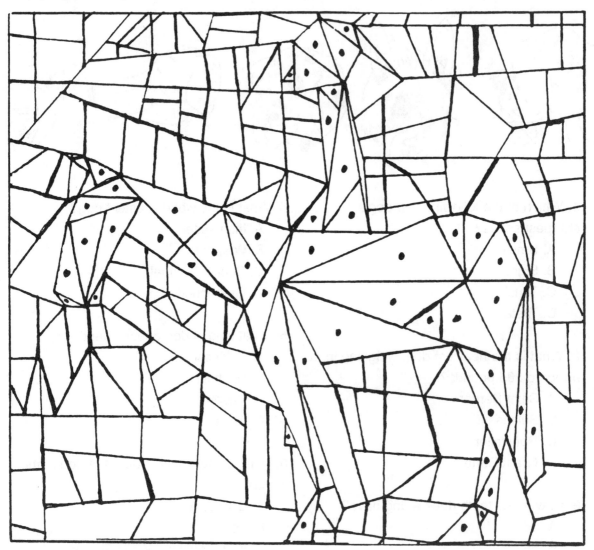

At the Store

The names of 12 things you can buy at the grocery store are hidden in the grid. Look across, down, and diagonally (on a slant). Circle each word as you find it and cross it off the list. We found EGGS for you. (Answers on page 141.)

WORD LIST

BACON	FLOUR	SALT
BREAD	JAM	SOUP
CHEESE	LETTUCE	SUGAR
~~EGGS~~	MILK	TEA

```
P  J  S  O  U  P  C
M  B  A  C  O  N  H
I  R  L  M  S  W  E
L  E  T  T  U  C  E
K  A  V (E  G  G  S)
H  D  N  Q  A  F  E
F  L  O  U  R  X  J
```

What's for Lunch?

*Each lunch food or drink will fit into 1 spot in the grid. We put some
letters in to get you started. (Answers on page 141.)*

WORD LIST

FRUIT

JUICE

MEATBALLS

MILK

PIZZA

SALAD

SANDWICH

SODA

SPAGHETTI

Crossword Puzzle

This crossword puzzle has a surprising twist because your clues are pictures instead of words.

WHAT YOU'LL NEED: graph paper; pencil; tracing paper; markers

Think of words to go in your crossword puzzle, making sure one word can connect with another word. Make your answer key using the graph paper. Draw a square for each letter of each word in your puzzle, connecting the words with a shared letter. Write each letter in. Then number each word going across and each word going down.

Cover the crossword puzzle with tracing paper to copy the squares without the letters in them, or redraw the puzzle without the letters on a new sheet of graph paper. Draw a clue for each word, and number the clues to match the word. If the word for 1 across is dog, then draw a dog for clue 1 across. Draw a decorative border around the puzzle. Make photocopies of the crossword puzzle to give to your friends and family.

Dog Days

Some of the things that dogs want are in the word list. Put each into the grid. We put some letters in to get you started. (Answers on page 141.)

WORD LIST

BASKET

BLANKET

BONE

BOWL

COLLAR

LEASH

TOY

International Signs

These international signs were designed to make travel easier for people who don't speak the same language. Can you guess what each sign means? (Answers on page 142.)

Going in Circles

Find the only path through the maze. (Answer on page 142.)

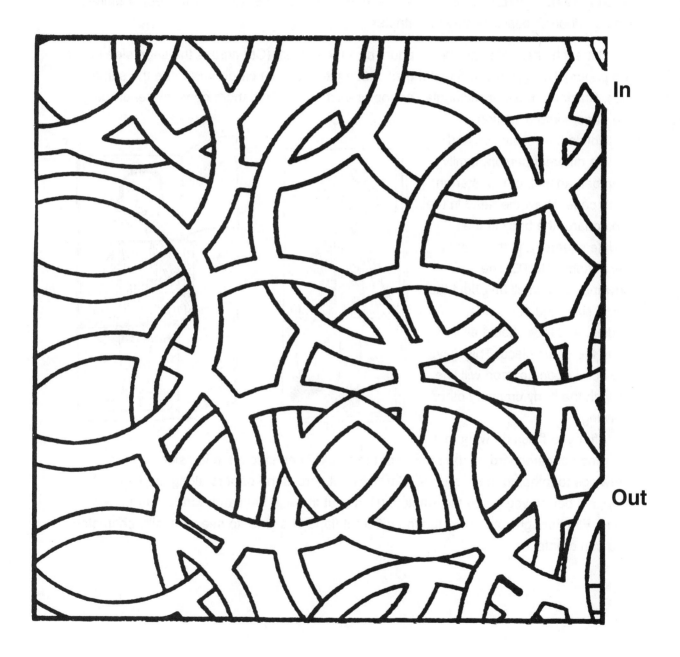

In

Out

Match-Up Books

Create your own collection of kooky characters.

YOU WILL NEED: scissors; 2 sheets of white paper (8½×11 inches); 1 piece of light cardboard; pencil or crayons; stapler

Cut each sheet of paper into 3 equal-size rectangles. (Cut across the short side of the paper.) This gives you 6 rectangles. Cut a piece of light cardboard to be the same size. Stack the 6 paper rectangles on top of each other. Fold them down twice, dividing the papers into 3 sections.

Unfold the rectangles and draw a different person, family member, animal, or monster on each page. Draw the head in the top square, the body in the middle square, and the legs at the bottom. (NOTE: The drawings should all be about the same size, and the heads, bodies, and legs should all line up in the same place. This way the head of one person will line up with the body on every other drawing.)

After you finish drawing, put the piece of cardboard on the bottom of the stack. Then staple the left side of your drawings together to make a book. Carefully cut across the papers along the folds, stopping before you get to the staples. (Don't cut through the cardboard!) Your book is done. Flip through your book, turning different flaps at a time, to see what silly characters you can create!

Mystery in China

Can you solve your way out of this mystery?

While traveling in China, you get into a tournament with the Chinese national Ping-Pong champion. The gym you're playing in is packed with people, and he's the best in the world. You're nervous, but all you need is 1 more point to beat him! On your final serve, you slam the ball so hard it misses the table, hits the ceiling, bounces on the floor, and rolls into a small drain that someone left uncovered in the corner. Unfortunately, it's the only ball you have.

"Who left this drain uncovered?" you ask. "The plumber," says the Ping-Pong champion. "The drain is clogged, so we called him to fix it. He went to get a special tool, and he won't be back for hours." You can see the Ping-Pong ball way down the drain, about 8 inches out of your reach. You must get the ball out quickly so you can try to win the tournament. The crowd in the bleachers won't wait long.

The only objects available to you are 2 Ping-Pong paddles, a small hand towel, 2 pitchers of water, 2 cups, and a stack of Ping-Pong rule books. How will you get the Ping-Pong ball? (Give up? See page 142.)

Road Sign Shapes

The writing from these signs has disappeared—can you tell what each one is just from its shape? (Answers on page 142.)

Volcano Maze

Help the scientist get down the mountain to his helicopter without crossing the lava flow. (Answer on page 142.)

Felt Story Boards

Turn a pizza box into a story board, and bring the story to life with felt pictures.

WHAT YOU'LL NEED: assorted colors of felt; scissors; clean, medium-size pizza box; craft glue; markers; trims such as pipe cleaners, straw, and yarn; plastic bags

To make the story board background, cut 2 pieces of dark-colored felt to fit the inside of the top and bottom of the pizza box. Apply a layer of glue to the inside of the box at the top and bottom. Place both felt background pieces down in the box over the glue. Let the glue set.

Using assorted colors of felt, cut out felt pieces to make a picture. For example, if you were telling the story *The Three Little Pigs,* you would need 3 pig cutouts, 1 wolf cutout, and 3 house cutouts. Draw the features with markers on the cut-out felt pieces. Draw the eyes, nose, and mouth on the pigs. Then glue a small piece of curled pipe cleaner for the tail, and glue on cutout felt overalls. Draw in the eyes, nose, mouth, and teeth on the wolf. Decorate each house with markers, felt, and other trims. Glue a bit of straw or some twigs on one house, and glue red felt bricks to another house. Place your pieces on the felt background to tell your story. When you're done playing, store each set of pieces in a plastic bag and place the bags in your pizza box.

Line Trace #1

Here's a picture that was made with one long line. The artist never picked up the pen when drawing it. Follow the line with your finger. Can you find the end of the line?

Golly Wolly

It's easy to make your own special riddles. Finding someone who can solve them is another matter!

Golly Wollys are riddles that you make up yourself. Just think of 2 words that rhyme (1 adjective and 1 noun), and you've found the answer. Let's use "big pig" as our example. Next, think of a clue that describes your rhyme. "Large hog" would work. So would "huge sow" or "giant oinker." Say your clue out loud to someone, and see if they can guess what your Golly Wolly is. Can you solve these Golly Wollys? (Answers on page 142.)

- Overweight tabby
- A home for animals that was just built yesterday
- Evening glow
- Fluffy white things that cause thunder
- An automobile that is many miles away
- A stinging insect that doesn't cost anything
- A round toy that is very high

State Match

Can you match the name of the state with its shape?

Sound easy? Well, you'd better be careful—some of the states are shown sideways, upside-down, or even reversed, as if you were seeing them in a mirror! (Answers on page 142.)

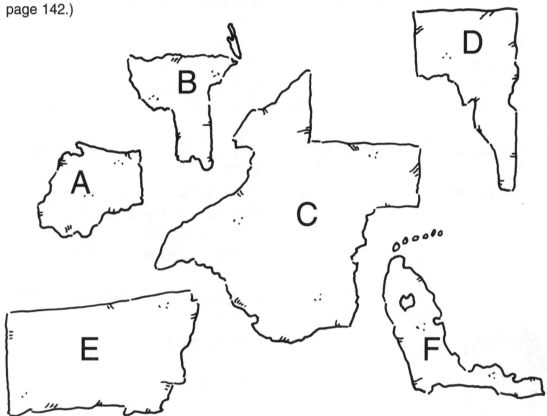

Inventors Quiz

How well do you know your inventors? (Answers on page 142.)

1. What did George Eastman invent in 1888?
   - A. Motorcycle
   - B. Test tube
   - C. Ice cream
   - D. Camera

2. What did Gail Borden invent in 1853?
   - A. Condensed milk
   - B. Cottage cheese
   - C. Yarn
   - D. Fluoride toothpaste

3. What did Clarence Birdseye invent in 1924?
   - A. Electricity
   - B. Wool underwear
   - C. Frozen food
   - D. Remote control

4. What did Charles Goodyear invent in 1839?
   - A. The blimp
   - B. A way to make rubber
   - C. Internal-combustion engine
   - D. Porcelain toilets

5. What did W. L. Judson invent in 1891?
   - A. Zipper
   - B. Shoelace
   - C. Pacifier
   - D. Freezer bags

6. What did Alfred Nobel invent in 1867?
   - A. Dynamite
   - B. Magnifying glass
   - C. Electric train
   - D. Skateboard

Eureka!

Mega Matchup

How quickly can you find the 3 pairs of matching squares in this puzzle? Careful, some squares are turned sideways. (Answers on page 143.)

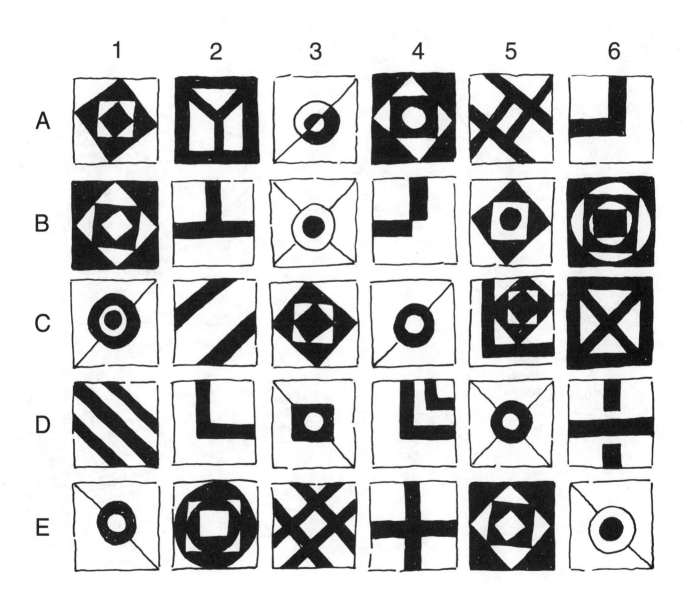

Avalanche Maze

Follow the path of footprints in this maze to help the mapmaker get to the cabin. Watch out for false leads! (Answer on page 143.)

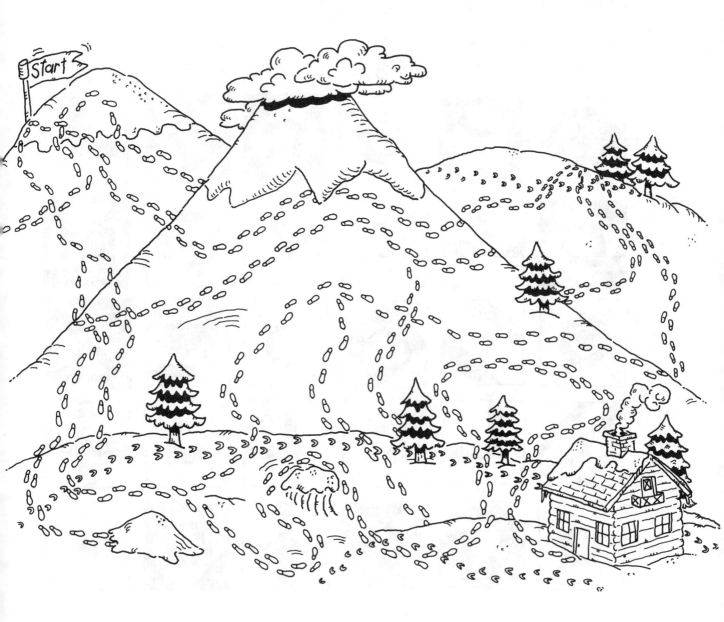

Space Shuttle Mystery

Can you solve your way way out of this mystery?

You are the captain of the U.S. *Constitution,* the country's newest space shuttle. It's your last day in orbit around the earth. After checking to make sure all systems are "Go," you line up the space vehicle with a nearby space station, where you will refuel for your journey back to Earth.

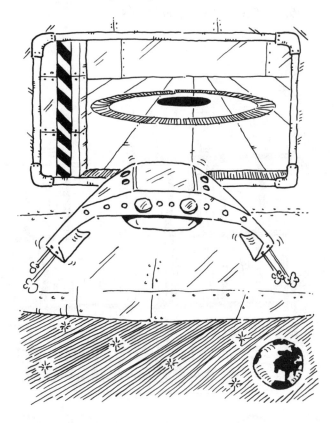

The space station's flight engineer directs you to a special docking bay where you are instructed to land. But when you get there, you realize that something is wrong. The space shuttle is too wide to get through the docking bay's doorway! After measuring the opening, you determine that it is exactly 4 inches too narrow.

You have to land the shuttle soon because your fuel supply is running low. The docking bay's door is made of strong metal, so you can't cut it. And you certainly can't cut anything off the shuttle. As you ponder your predicament, you notice that the shuttle's fuel light has turned on. How will you ever get the shuttle into the space station? (Give up? See page 143.)

Pirate Ship Maze

Find the shortest route from the deck of the ship to the hidden chest below. (Answer on page 143.)

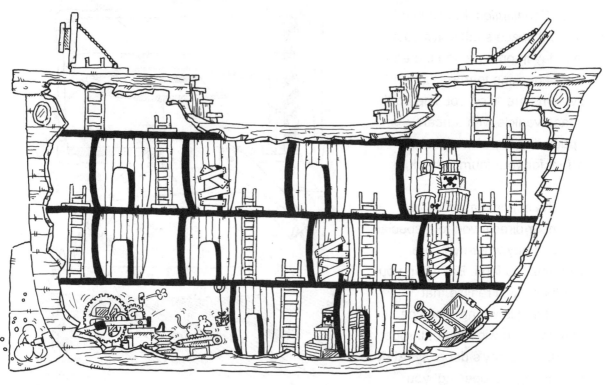

Travel Trivia

Where would you use these things to travel? (Answers on page 143.)

1.	Gondola	A.	Dominican Republic
2.	Sleigh	B.	England
3.	Kayak	C.	Italy
4.	Rickshaw	D.	France
5.	Sampan	E.	Alaska
6.	Lorry	F.	Peru
7.	Motovelo	G.	Japan
8.	Zeppelin	H.	China
9.	Motoconcho	I.	Norway
10.	Alpaca	J.	Germany

Line Trace #2

Here's another picture that was made with one long line. The artist never picked up his pen when drawing it. Follow the line with your finger. Can you find the end of the line?

Zoo Babies

Can you match the animal in Column 1 with its baby name in Column 2? (Answers on page 143.)

COLUMN 1	COLUMN 2
tiger	eaglet
cow	poult
seal	joey
horse	fawn
kangaroo	cygnet
eagle	gosling
goose	kitten
swan	foal
turkey	chick
deer	whelp
rooster	calf

Road Map Mystery

Follow each person's path on the map of town, and answer the questions below. (Answers on page 143.)

1. Who visited the post office twice?
2. Who went from the bank to the hospital?
3. Who visited the most places?
4. Who visited the fewest places?
5. Where did Bill go between the hospital and school?

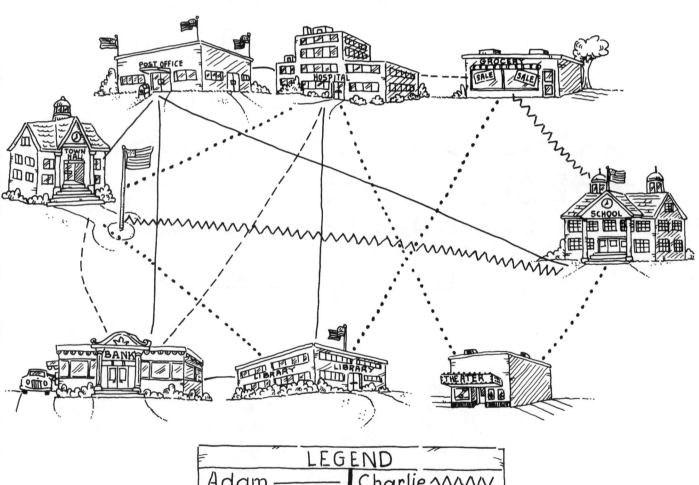

LEGEND

Adam ————	Charlie ᐯᐯᐯᐯ
Bill ··········	Don – – – – –

Picture Puns

Draw pictures that stand for a word. Have your friends and family guess the words!

WHAT YOU'LL NEED: 8 to 11 sheets of drawing paper; markers; stapler

Draw 2 pictures that stand for a word on a sheet of drawing paper. You might choose the word snowman and draw snowflakes and a man, or you might choose the word starfish and draw a star and a fish. Write the word on the back of the paper. Make 8 to 10 picture puns. Make a book out of your drawings. Decorate a sheet of drawing paper for the cover. Set all the pages together and staple the top of the pages to bind your book. Show your book to family members and see if they can guess your words.

Try other picture puns with homonyms. These are words that sound alike but have different spellings and meanings. Some examples are aunt and ant; rein, reign, and rain; and cache and cash. Draw as many as you can and add them to your book.

• • • • • • • • • • • • • • • • • • • •

Ancient Egypt Rebus

Can you figure out the rebus below? Read the pictures as if they were words. (Answer on page 144.)

When explorers found Tut's , they couldn't

believe their . They found a golden , a giant

made of marble, and made of , and more

and than they could count.

True or False

You'll need at least 3 players to make this fun game work.

WHAT YOU'LL NEED: several sheets of notebook or other paper; 3 pens or pencils

Each player gets 1 sheet of paper and 1 pen or pencil. Without talking to each other, each player must think of 10 true-or-false statements to quiz the other 2 players with. Statements can cover subjects currently in the news, things you've learned in school, sports—just about anything, as long as they can be answered with a simple "True" or "False."

Player 1 goes first. He or she begins by reading the first true-or-false statement to Player 2. After Player 2 responds, Player 3 has to agree or disagree with Player 2's answer. If Player 2 was right and Player 3 was wrong, Player 2 gets 10 points. If Player 2 was wrong but Player 3 was right, Player 3 gets 10 points. If both players were right, each gets 5 points.

Player 1's second true-or-false statement goes to Player 3; this time, Player 2 must agree or disagree. Player 1 continues alternating between Players 2 and 3 this way until the quiz is finished. The player with the highest score wins the round.

When Player 1 is finished, it's Player 2's turn to quiz Players 1 and 3 the same way. Then Player 3 quizzes Players 1 and 2. The person with the highest overall score wins.

Haunted House Maze

There's only one good way out of a haunted house—as fast as possible! (Answer on page 144.)

You're trapped on the roof of a haunted house, and you have to find your way through the house and out through the front door. Watch where you're going. Some rooms and stairs lead to dead ends—or worse!

Sports Trivia

Test your knowledge of sports. (Answers on page 144.)

1. In baseball, how many players are on the diamond when the other team is at bat?

    A. 7
    B. 8
    C. 9
    D. 10

2. The Olympics started more than 100 years ago in 1896. What city hosted the first Games?

    A. Athens, Greece
    B. Rome, Italy
    C. Atlanta, Georgia
    D. Paris, France

3. In what country was ice hockey invented?

    A. United States
    B. Norway
    C. Iceland
    D. Canada

4. Which of these is NOT a sport in the Summer Olympics?

    A. Canoeing
    B. Pole vaulting
    C. Bowling
    D. Badminton

5. The largest fish ever officially caught on a rod weighed 2,664 pounds. That's over 2½ tons—heavier than your car! What kind of fish was it?

    A. Blue whale
    B. Great white shark
    C. Giant tuna
    D. Minnow

6. Which of these sports is NOT played with a stick or racket?

    A. Lacrosse
    B. Jai Alai
    C. Croquet
    D. Rugby

Crossed Words

You can make your own crossword puzzle for 2 by playing this word-linking game.

WHAT YOU'LL NEED: paper (graph paper works best); pencil; ruler

Mark off a square that contains 15 boxes down and 15 across. Graph paper works best, but if you don't have any, use a ruler to draw the lines on a piece of blank paper. Outline the box in the very center of the puzzle so that it stands out.

Choose a theme for your puzzle, such as animals, flowers, countries, sports, fruits, vegetables, and so on. Player 1 thinks of a word that fits into the chosen category. Then he or she writes the word on the page, 1 letter per box. The first word must have at least 1 letter that goes through the middle box.

Players take turns thinking of words and writing them down. The tricky part is that every word must share a letter with a word that's already on the page. Score 1 point for each letter in a word—but don't count any letters you "borrow" from another word. Play until nobody can think of any more words that will fit on the graph. Highest score wins.

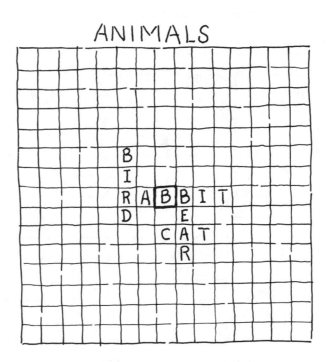

ANIMALS

Box Maze

Make 2 box mazes and have races with a friend. If you can finish without losing your marbles, you win.

WHAT YOU'LL NEED: drawing paper; pencil; markers; scissors; shoe box with lid; craft glue; small marble

Practice drawing a maze design on a piece of paper. Think of a theme for your maze. For example, it might be a swamp game such as "Watch Out for the Alligator Ponds." Draw lines for the maze walls, and mark places along the maze to cut holes (the ponds) for the marble to fall through. Mark the starting and finishing points of the maze. Once you've created a design you like, draw the maze lines and hole marks on the inside of the shoe box lid. Cut the pond holes where indicated. Make sure the holes are slightly larger than the marble. Decorate the maze with markers. To make the maze walls, cut ½-inch-wide strips of cardboard from the rest of the shoe box. The strips should be the length of each maze line. Apply glue along the lines in the lid, and stand a cardboard strip in the glue to make each wall. Let the glue dry. To play, place a marble at the starting point. Then tilt and turn the lid to move the marble along the maze to the finishing point. Be sure to watch out for the alligator pond holes!

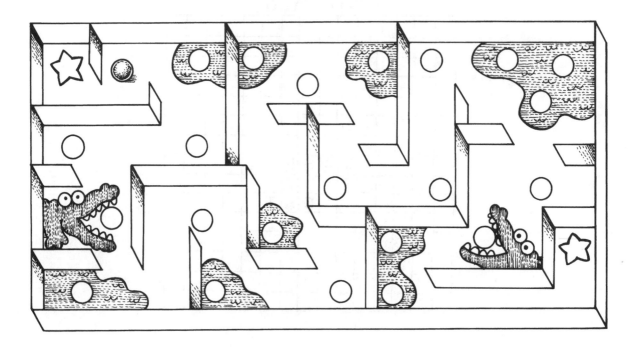

Riddlemaker

It's easy to make your own riddles—if you just know a few easy tricks of the riddler's trade.

Think of something you want to make a riddle about. We'll do pigs as an example, because pigs are pretty funny creatures. Make a list of all the words you can think of that have to do with pigs. You might think of mud, hog, pork, bacon, and ham. Next, think of a pun you can make by rhyming one of those words with some other word. For example, "hog" rhymes with "dog."

Now put on your riddler's cap and think of a well-known saying, song, or phrase that has the word "dog" in it. For example, "It's raining cats and dogs." By switching the word "dog" for the word "hog," we have the answer to our riddle: "It's raining cats and hogs." Now we have to think of the riddle itself. How about this: "What does a pig say during a thunderstorm?" That's right: "It's raining cats and hogs!"

Here's another pig riddle using the word "pork": What is a pig's favorite town? Give up? New Pork City! See how many riddles you can make up.

Chalkboard Rebus

In a rebus, you read pictures as if they were words. Can you figure out the rebus below? (Answer on page 144.)

Dear Class,

Your T+🪑 can 🪢 🐝 at 🏫 today. H+👂 is your

assignment. Please ✋ it in 🐝+4 three o'🕐 . Write a story about

a 🐋, a 🦭 , and a 👔 +ger.

Cat Quiz

Here's a trivia quiz that's purr-fect for cat lovers. (Answers on page 144.)

1. What cat is the fastest animal in the world, running up to 70 miles per hour?
   A. Cheetah
   B. Tomcat
   C. Bengal tiger
   D. Black panther

2. Which 2 members of the cat family don't climb?
   A. Lion and cheetah
   B. Tiger and cheetah
   C. Lion and tiger
   D. Panther and lion

3. Which part of a cat is stronger than any other animals'?
   A. Tooth
   B. Tail
   C. Rib
   D. Claw

4. Which of the following is NOT a member of the cat family?
   A. Lion
   B. Polecat
   C. Tiger
   D. Siamese

5. The Cheshire Cat could slowly disappear, leaving only its smile behind. In what book can you read about this magical cat?
   A. *Cat's Cradle*
   B. *Harriet the Spy*
   C. *Witches' Brew*
   D. *Alice In Wonderland*

6. What famous words does cartoon character Sylvester the Cat always say?
   A. "Exit, stage left!"
   B. "To the rescue!"
   C. "Sufferin' succotash!"
   D. "Cowabunga, dude!"

Wacky Words

Have you ever heard someone try to finish a joke or a story—but fail because he or she couldn't think of the right word?

If you have, you might enjoy making up wacky word stories for other people. All you need to do is write your own story and leave out some of the words. Make a note of what kind of word or part of speech the missing word is. Then ask your friends to "fill in the blanks" before they hear the story.

Below are the first few sentences of a wacky word story. Before you read it aloud, go through it and ask the other players to give you a word that fits each requirement (in parentheses). In the sample below, you would say, "Give me a boy's name." Write down

the word you are given. Next you would say, "Give me an adjective." Write down the word. Do the same thing for the rest of the story. When you have all the words you need, read the story out loud, putting the words you were given into the right places. You won't believe some of the wacky stories you'll get!

Once there was a Prince named (boy's name) who was very (adjective). The Prince loved to play practical jokes. Who can forget the time he surprised Queen (woman's name) with a big, fat (noun) that he hid in her (noun)? We all (verb ending in "-ed") for days!

Rebus Story

In a rebus, you read pictures as if they were words. The next time friends come to play, ask everyone to make one rebus story. Then everyone gives their own story to someone else to tell.

WHAT YOU'LL NEED: black felt-tip pen; drawing paper; markers

Create a story with pictures for words. You can make up your own story or use your favorite fairy tale. Write your story on a piece of paper. As you write it down, draw certain words, especially repeated words, as a picture. For example, if you wrote a story about a king, you could draw a picture of a crown as the symbol for the word king. Write and draw a whole story, and bind the pieces of paper together to make a book. (See page 72 or 78 for binding instructions.)

Dictionary

The object of the game is to figure out the word by listening to its definition.

WHAT YOU'LL NEED: pocket dictionary

First, let all the players know how many pages are in the dictionary you will be using. The reader holds the dictionary and says, "Which page?" Someone else calls out a page number. The reader then turns to that page and asks, "Which column?" (Smaller dictionaries may have 1 column on a page instead of 2. If your dictionary has just 1 column, skip this step.) Someone calls out left or right.

Finally, the reader asks, "How many?" Someone calls out a number from 1 to 10. From the top of the page, the reader counts down that many words and reads the definition out loud. Everyone else tries to guess what the word is. If no one can guess, you may give clues. For example, you could tell them the first letter of the word, or you could read the definition of the word above or below the chosen word. The player who guesses correctly becomes the reader. If no one guesses, start the game again with a new word.

Wildlife Trivia

You may already know that a cat is a feline and a dog is a canine, but what about these other animals? Match the animal with the word that describes it. (Answers on page 144.)

1. apian   A. bull
2. avian   B. bear
3. bovine   C. sheep
4. equine   D. lion
5. leonine   E. ape
6. lupine   F. wolf
7. ovine   G. horse
8. simian   H. cow
9. taurine   I. bee
10. ursine   J. bird

Find the Presents

In this game of strategy, race your opponent to locate the hidden presents.

WHAT YOU'LL NEED: drawing paper; ruler; markers; scissors; construction paper

To make the game board, draw an 8×8-inch square on a piece of drawing paper. Divide the square into 64 squares, 1 inch each, by drawing lines 1 inch apart down and across. There should be 8 squares down each side. Label the rows across A through H and label the columns down 1 through 8 as shown. Take your original to a copy center and make 4 copies—you'll need 4 copies to play 1 game. (Save your original game board to make more copies later.)

On a piece of construction paper, draw 10 presents. Make four 1×2-inch presents and six 1×1-inch presents. Decorate your presents and cut them out. Each player gets 2 large presents, 3 small ones, and 2 game boards.

To play the game, arrange your presents on 1 game board. Then take turns guessing the location of your opponent's presents by calling out the name of the square. For example, you might ask if the present is in E-3. If the answer is no, mark the E-3 spot on your blank game board with an X; if the answer is yes, mark it with a star. Then your friend takes a turn. The first person to find all the presents wins.

Morse Code

Once you know the code, you can make words out of dots and dashes.

Back in 1838, Samuel Morse created a special code that was named after him. In his code, a dot is a short tap and a dash is a long tap (with more time in between taps, that is). People used his code to send messages before telephones or radios were invented.

Morse designed his code so that the most often used letters in the alphabet have the shortest signals. Tap out your own messages in Morse Code on your knee. A short tap for the dots, a longer tap for the dashes. Have your friend write out your message and read it back to you. Take turns.

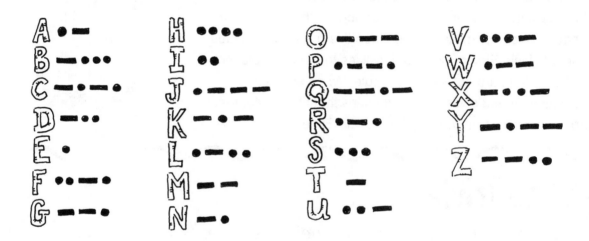

Uncle Elmer

Just about everyone has someone in their family who is a little different, but Uncle Elmer is special.

Uncle Elmer is a strange old guy. He only likes certain things. For example, he like apples, but he doesn't like oranges. He likes ladders, but he doesn't like steps. He likes butter, but he doesn't like margarine. Can you guess why? Because Uncle Elmer only likes words with double letters!

To play Uncle Elmer, one player silently decides what really makes Uncle Elmer unusual. Perhaps he only likes words with the letter E in them, or objects that are red, or have wheels, or make noises. Then this player gives clues about Uncle Elmer's likes and dislikes to the other players, who try to figure out the special rule. When someone catches on and gives a few examples that fit the rule, that person gets a turn talking about Uncle Elmer.

State Trivia

Match the following states with their nickname. (Answers on page 144.)

1. Old Line State	A. Mississippi
2. Palmetto State	B. Indiana
3. Granite State	C. Arkansas
4. Hoosier State	D. California
5. Magnolia State	E. Maryland
6. Land of Opportunity	F. South Carolina
7. Golden State	G. North Dakota
8. Sagebrush State	H. Nevada
9. Peace Garden State	I. Utah
10. Beehive State	J. New Hampshire

Geography Quiz

Test yourself to see how much you know about the world around you. (Answers on page 144.)

1. At 20,320 feet, this is the highest mountain in the United States.
   - A. Mount St. Helens
   - B. Mount Rainier
   - C. Mount McKinley
   - D. Pikes Peak

2. At 4,180 miles, this is the longest river in the world.
   - A. Nile River
   - B. Tigris River
   - C. Mississippi River
   - D. Amazon River

3. At 29,028 feet, this is the highest mountain in the world.
   - A. Mount Rushmore
   - B. Mount Everest
   - C. Kilimanjaro
   - D. Mount Washington

4. At 3,212 feet, this is the highest waterfall on earth.
   - A. Angel Falls, Venezuela
   - B. Niagara Falls, New York
   - C. Clifty Falls, Indiana
   - D. Bushkill Falls, Pennsylvania

5. At 3,212 square miles, this is the world's largest freshwater lake.
   - A. Lake Superior
   - B. Lake Okeechobee
   - C. Lake Michigan
   - D. Lake Huron

6. Mammoth Caves National Park—the largest cave system in the world, with more than 300 miles of tunnels—stays at what temperature year-round?
   - A. 85 degrees
   - B. 69 degrees
   - C. 54 degrees
   - D. 30 degrees

Balloon Badminton

Mom always said not to play ball in the house—until she learned this fun indoor game.

WHAT YOU'LL NEED: craft glue; 2 craft sticks; 2 plastic coffee can lids; markers; newspaper; scissors; string or yarn; balloons

Glue a craft stick to each plastic coffee can lid to make the badminton rackets. Use markers to decorate your rackets with opposing pictures. You might draw a sun on one and a moon on another, or an elephant and a mouse, or a red and green light.

To make the net, fan-fold a sheet of newspaper. Cut out V-sections as shown. Open the paper and thread some string through the top row of the cutouts. Tie the net to 2 chairs. Blow up a balloon, and play a slow-motion, fun game of badminton inside the house. If you want, decorate the balloon to match your rackets. You might draw a star, a peanut, or a yellow light.

Scramblers

Answers from page 92.

A) TRAP. B) GIGGLE. C) BRACE.
D) LUCKY. Answer to riddle:
GARBAGE TRUCK.

Happy Birthday!

Answers from page 94.

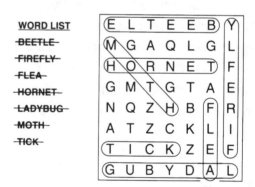

Outer Space Trivia

Answers from page 95.
1) D. 2) A. 3) C. 4) D. 5) C. 6) B.

Don't Bug Me!

Answers from page 96.

Perspectives

Answer from page 96.
Pyramid No. 3 matches the original,
except that it is shown from the side
instead of from above.

Mystery in England

Answer from page 97.
Stack the encyclopedias so you can
climb them and reach the key.

Color Fun
Answers from page 97.

~~BLACK~~   ~~ORANGE~~
~~BLUE~~   ~~RED~~
~~BROWN~~   ~~WHITE~~
~~GREEN~~   ~~YELLOW~~

```
        G       Y
      O R A N G E
        E       L
B L U E   B L A C K
R       N       O
O       R       W
W H I T E
N       D
```

True or False
Answers from page 98.

	TRUE	FALSE
Z is the first letter of the alphabet.	E	(A)
Carrots are orange.	(R)	S
January is the first month.	(I)	U
A baby cat is a kitten.	(Z)	B
Shoes are worn on the hands.	I	(O)
Marbles are square.	G	(N)
1 + 1 = 3	O	(A)

Mystery in India
Answer from page 98.

Take the swan across the river first. Then go back and get the tiger. Drop the tiger off on the other side, but before you leave, pick up the swan again. Carry the swan back across the river, and drop it off. Pick up the cashews and carry them across the river. Then come back and get the swan.

Creature Quiz
Answers from page 99.

1) C. 2) A. 3) B. 4) B. 5) A. 6) C.

Tool Kit
Answers from page 100.

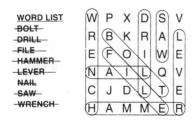

WORD LIST
~~BOLT~~
~~DRILL~~
~~FILE~~
~~HAMMER~~
~~LEVER~~
NAIL
~~SAW~~
~~WRENCH~~

Box Count
Answer from page 100.

Total number of boxes is 79.

Blocks Galore
Answer from page 101.

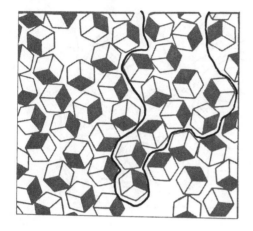

Fill In
Answer from page 104.

What's for Lunch?
Answers from page106.

WORD LIST
- ~~FRUIT~~
- ~~JUICE~~
- ~~MEATBALLS~~
- ~~MILK~~
- ~~PIZZA~~
- ~~SALAD~~
- ~~SANDWICH~~
- ~~SODA~~
- ~~SPAGHETTI~~

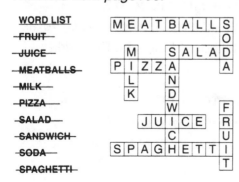

Whose Kite Am I?
Answers from page 102.
From left to right, the kites in the air belong to Pat, Ron, Debra, and Jill.

Dog Quiz
Answers from page 103.
1) A. 2) A. 3) C. 4) D. 5) C. 6) D.

At the Store
Answers from page 105.

WORD LIST
- ~~BACON~~
- ~~BREAD~~
- ~~CHEESE~~
- ~~EGGS~~
- ~~FLOUR~~
- ~~JAM~~
- ~~LETTUCE~~
- ~~MILK~~
- ~~SALT~~
- ~~SOUP~~
- ~~SUGAR~~
- ~~TEA~~

Dog Days
Answers from page 108.

WORD LIST
- ~~BASKET~~
- ~~BLANKET~~
- ~~BONE~~
- ~~BOWL~~
- ~~COLLAR~~
- ~~LEASH~~
- ~~TOY~~

International Signs

Answers from page 108.

Top row, left to right: lost & found, currency exchange, falling rocks, drinking water, no entry. Bottom row, left to right: gift shop, information, viewing area, Customs, hiking trail.

Going in Circles

Answer from page 109.

Mystery in China

Answer from page 111.

Pour the pitcher of water down the drain. Because the drain is clogged, the water will rise, bringing the Ping-Pong ball up with it.

Volcano Maze

Answer from page 112.

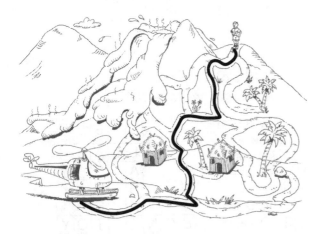

Road Sign Shapes

Answers from page 111.

Top row, left to right: stop, yield, one way, do not enter. Bottom row, left to right: railroad crossing, interstate route, U.S. route, state route.

Golly Wolly

Answers from page 114.

Fat cat, new zoo, night light, loud cloud, far car, free bee, tall ball.

State Match

Answers from page 115.

A) Wisconsin. B) New York. C) Texas. D) Idaho. E) Montana. F) Florida.

Inventors Quiz

Answers from page 116.

1) D. 2) A. 3) C. 4) B. 5) A. 6) A.

Mega Matchup

Answers from page 117.

Matching pairs: A6 and D2, C4 and E1, B1 and E5.

Avalanche Maze

Answer from page 118.

Space Shuttle Mystery

Answer from page 119.

Instead of flying straight in, you'll have to angle the shuttle diagonally to make it through the doorway.

Pirate Ship Maze

Answer from page 120.

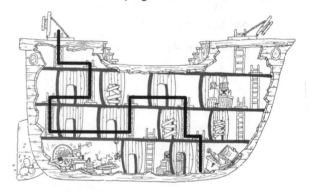

Travel Trivia

Answers from page 120.

1) C. 2) I. 3) E. 4) G. 5) H. 6) B. 7) D. 8) J. 9) A. 10) F.

Zoo Babies

Answers from page 121.

Tiger: kitten; cow: calf; seal: whelp; horse: foal; kangaroo: joey; eagle: eaglet; goose: gosling; swan: cygnet; turkey: poult; deer: fawn; rooster: chick.

Road Map Mystery

Answers from page 122.

1) Adam. 2) Don. 3) Bill. 4) Charlie. 5) Theater.

Ancient Egypt Rebus

Answer from page 124.

When explorers found KING Tut's GRAVE, they couldn't believe their EYES. They found a golden BOAT, a giant CAT made of marble, PLATES and CUPS made of WOOD, and more COINS and DIAMONDS than they could count.

Haunted House Maze

Answer from page 125.

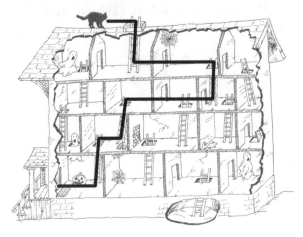

Sports Trivia

Answers from page 126.

1) C. 2) A. 3) D. 4) C. 5) A. 6) D.

Chalkboard Rebus

Answer from page 129.

Dear Class, Your T+CHAIR [teacher] can KNOT BEE at SCHOOL today. H+EAR [here] is your assignment. Please HAND it in BEE+4 [before] three o'CLOCK. Write a story about a WHALE, a WALRUS, and a TIE+ger [tiger].

Cat Quiz

Answers from page 130.

1) A. 2) C. 3) D. 4) B. 5) D. 6) C.

Wildlife Trivia

Answers from page 133.

1) I. 2) J. 3) H. 4) G. 5) D. 6) F. 7) C. 8) E. 9) A. 10) B.

State Trivia

Answers from page 136.

1) E. 2) F. 3) J. 4) B. 5) A. 6) C. 7) D. 8) H. 9) G. 10) I.

Geography Quiz

Answers from page 137.

1) C. 2) A. 3) B. 4) A. 5) A. 6) C.